The Image of God/ The Likeness of Men

ROBERT MCCLERREN

BALBOA.
PRESS
A DIVISION OF HAY HOUSE

Scripture quotations marked KJV are from the Holy Bible, King James Version (Authorized Version). First published in 1611. Quoted from the KJV Classic Reference Bible, Copyright © 1983 by The Zondervan Corporation.

Balboa Press books may be ordered through booksellers or by contacting:

Balboa Press
A Division of Hay House
1663 Liberty Drive
Bloomington, IN 47403
www.balboapress.com
1 (877) 407-4847

Print information available on the last page.

ISBN: 978-1-5043-4797-6 (sc)
ISBN: 978-1-5043-4799-0 (hc)
ISBN: 978-1-5043-4798-3 (e)

Library of Congress Control Number: 2015921041

Balboa Press rev. date: 05/05/2016

CONTENTS

Foreword vii

Chapter 1   Man's Identity 1
Chapter 2   The Symbiotic Relationship Of God And Man 9
Chapter 3   The Reflection of God 47
Chapter 4   The Trifecta of God's and Man's Attributes 149
Chapter 5   Contemplative Prayer 183
Chapter 6   Bringing Reality to Mind 191

FOREWORD

As a young man working in my father's plumbing shop, it was my good fortune to work beside some men who had recently emigrated from a war-torn Germany, and a few who had been here from before the war, but who had been trained there as young men before coming here. Some had even served in Germany's army as plumbers working on steam engines for their war effort. One such man was Joe Schaefer who insisted his name was pronounced "sheefer and not shafer". He had one other language quirk – he mixed his idioms up a bit in that when something surprising occurred, he would say, ". . . one of a sudden – such and such happened", instead of "All of a sudden, or Suddenly. . .!!"

Well, this small mighty volume by one of my students, Robert McClerren, is a "one of a sudden" kind of phenomenon. Here is a source for pastors, preachers, and church leaders who find themselves all too often in need of a topic, or even a series of topics for a sermon, or series of sermons; classes or even workshops. Here is a ready reference in the familiar KJV affirming the truth on every page that somehow, in some degree or other, we are created in the Imago Dei and therefore possess the same qualities in varying degrees as the very Pattern from which we are drawn.

For those who feel there is a bit more "proof-texting" than exegetical substance, one merely need to read the larger pericope surrounding each text and thus avoid the usual tendency towards eisegesis which is the normal result of topic-hunting, or the proof-texting of one's personal agenda rather than what God has in store for those who are willing to dig a bit further.

This volume is unique in that it is a first work by this author, and that it comes from the heart of a pastor whose only desire is to uplift the consciousness and awareness of his congregation. His great desire is that those who read and use the information found herein will find themselves transported to a place where their faith began, or forward into a greater sense of who they are and "Whose" they truly are with all the rights and privileges pertaining thereto as reconciled children of God living in the Kingdom of their Father (Luke 17:21). Perhaps in some small or very large way, this book will encourage its readers to accept the reconciliation of the cross and begin to experience the salvation (spiritual health) promised by living the life of Christ as only those who are able acknowledge their "Imago Dei" (Romans 5:10).

Congratulations, Robert, and thank you for bringing such a truth to those who are willing to know the Truth of God that does genuinely set us all on the pathway to personal and corporate freedom in, of, by, through, and for God. And all are Blessed!!

All the best to all who read and take to heart the message of this book.
William H. Ward, B.A., M.A., M.Div., Ph.D.

CHAPTER 1
Man's Identity

When we read in the Bible that man was created in the image of God, it evokes questions in the mind of man. What kind of image? Why would God create me in His image? What qualities do I have that are this image of God? When we look into a mirror, we are faced with an image of ourselves. Is it the human form with all its facial features that God is referring to?

Using the word "image" certainly suggests it is a quality that can be appreciated through sight. Perhaps this is too literal, as the Bible often speaks in terms of metaphor. If so, we are not looking for a physical equivalent, but one that is spiritual. The Bible clearly states that God is Spirit. It is also recorded that God made man a living soul. Of all creation, it is only said of God that He breathed into man the breath of life. While God spoke the world and all that is in it into existence, He reserved a unique and spiritual transference of Himself in creating man. Man has a spiritual bond with God that is unlike any other creature in heaven or earth. It is the Spirit of God that gave man life. It is God's Spirit that speaks to our spirit. Man is the sole object and recipient of God's love. Without man, God would have no way to communicate his love. Man is indeed created in the image of God.

The image of God

So God created man in his own image, in the image of God created he him; male and female created he them.

Genesis 1:27

In whom the god of this world hath blinded the minds of them which believe not, lest the light of the glorious gospel of Christ, who is the image of God, should shine unto them.

2 Corinthians 4:4

The likeness of men

For what the law could not do, in that it was weak through the flesh, God sending his own Son in the likeness of sinful flesh, and for sin, condemned sin in the flesh:

Romans 8:3

But made himself of no reputation, and took upon him the form of a servant, and was made in the likeness of men:

Philippians 2:7

For he hath made him to be sin for us, who knew no sin; that we might be made the righteousness of God in him.

2 Corinthians 5:21

Discovering Self

In the 1960s there was a question that seemed to permeate the minds of young people. It was an effort to discover oneself that was adopted by the hippy culture, or at least by those who opposed prevailing thought about man and the society in which he lived. There were phrases used such as anti-establishment. These new ideals tested the very fabric of our society. "I need to discover myself." The statement at the time seemed frivolous even ludicrous, but it was also very telling of what was going on in the minds of young people.

With Judean-Christian foundations being challenged in academia, individuals were confronted with questions about their own existence. They had been indoctrinated by evolutionary thought. They have been told their lives were nothing more than a product of time, energy and chance. They were now forced to rely on a tenuous explanation for their existence: one that denied divine intervention. What possible meaning of life could there be in an existence that emerged from disorder, let alone the absence of divine love?

Years later we see the same yearning for identity show itself as an introduction in a political campaign. The first words uttered by United States Navy Vice Admiral James Stockdale, when it was announced during the 1992 presidential campaign that he was Ross Perot's VP running mate was "Who am I, Why am I here?" That was most certainly a question on the minds of those waiting to learn more about his qualifications and political agenda. Politics aside, these two questions have most certainly been at the forefront of mans mind, throughout the ages. In order to best understand who we are and why we are here, we must first understand who God is and how we fit in Gods creation.

Understanding who God is, is not just a nice thing to know. Knowing God is everything. It is only when we know God that we can begin to put all aspects of life in proper perspective. In developing our understanding of God, we need to guard against adopting false teachings: attributes that are not God's.

Don't be afraid of what you might discover. We need to take care not to deny who God is, simply because it does not fit a popular preconceived notion. Knowing God's attributes, and denying them in your life is tantamount to blasphemy. The more we know God, the greater our influence for good will be. It behooves us to allow the truth of who God is to guide our thinking and ultimately our lives.

In Christian fundamentalism it is common to evangelize with an opening question such as: "If you were to die today, are you 100 % sure you would go to heaven?" Answering with anything other than a resounding yes, gives the "soul winner" cause to proceed to proselytize. The goal is to convince people their soul is in danger of eternal damnation, and you can lead them in a prayer that will prevent this. That's one of the driving forces that keeps Christian fundamentalism on the march.

Wouldn't it be tragic, if that's all there were to life? Many Christians live as if they are biding their time on earth until the Lord calls them home to be with Him. They have acquired their fire insurance but don't much care for the world they live in. They are highly critical of others who are different; indicating they are not up to the standards of the elect. There is even a type of snob factor displayed among those in mainline denominations. They know better. Yet their lackluster faith has provided them with no more prowess than claiming membership in doctrinarian social clubs aka church.

Universal Desires

Both religious and non-religious people believe the world should be a better place than it is. The quandary is, with so many working to that end, why isn't the world a better place? There is no difficulty identifying problems. There is no complacency in understanding needs. Yet too many are in a state of denial when it comes to their responsibility to effect the world for Good. The religious are too pious to admit contributing to the current state of affairs. They seem to be saying, "I didn't make the mess, and it's not my job to clean it up." "It's those sinners who are ruining it for everyone." "If there were only a way to convince those people to become believers, like me, things would be different." To avoid conflict, we adopt such notions as: "agreeing to disagree," which only provides a pseudo type of contentment. It assures us that a certain level of civility will be maintained. We now can have any number of conversations and remain comfortable. No resolution or consensus is required. Anything beyond this requires action, and action requires effort. And everyone knows getting involved with anything new can be a messy proposition. The real indictment of the religious faithful is; they are genuinely clueless how to effect change.

Too many individuals live as though no particular effort to improve, on their part, is required. "I have made my profession of faith" "I attend church services regularly." "I am a law abiding person." "I have learned religious speak." "I will just sit quietly with my pious thoughts, snub my neighbors and wait to be rescued from this immoral world full of injustices."

Is championing the eternal destiny of others enough? Is this truly what the Lord requires? Is it really a valid excuse for ignoring the here and now? As precious as the soul of man is, we also have an obligation to life that is all around us. The world we live in needs our attention now. It cannot wait until death, to be assured of a better tomorrow.

The Product of Secularism

The human condition has been one of a struggle for survival: fraught with conflict, adversity and oppression. Philosophers have called upon human reason to bring meaning and order to life. Religions have reminded us of our moral and ethical duties to mankind. Political leaders have sought to organize societies in the name of liberty and justice for all. Legislatures have given us laws in an attempt to criminalize bad behavior. In turn, law enforcement works to punish those who break those laws to protect us from harm. Technology has progressed through the centuries, to offer us the most advanced and luxurious lifestyles ever. And yet with all these gains, humanity is no more moral or godly than it was 2000 years ago. Humanity has just become more adept at hiding its deficiencies and lack of integrity by burying them in its ITT toys. They may appear as gaps in tape recordings, erased hard drives, missing e-mails, e-mail and social media accounts set up with pseudonyms, the misuse of private servers, or sexting, all devised to obfuscate the truth. These behaviors are no more palpable than Adam and Eve's disobedience to God, their denial: an attempt to hide their nakedness.

Today, criminals and law enforcement are on a parallel course with technology; engaged in a race of one-upmanship. Dictators with their egotistical ambitions seek the conquest of other peoples and lands. Militaries of the world are at work developing more efficient and effective killing machines. Lawmakers are at work passing laws to curb the rise of criminal behavior. The ranks of law enforcement grow and increase their capabilities each year. Much is done in an attempt to stave rising crime rates. The growing number of criminals being incarcerated has not kept us safe. There are an estimated 2,266,800 now behind bars, an increase of 1,891,900 over the past 50 years.

Excuses abound

We excuse criminals, suggesting that their economic status is cause for bad behavior. Stealing from someone is not an indication of an economic problem but rather a moral deficiency. When Jesus admonished us to "Love your neighbor as yourself" it was with the idea of "do no harm." Loving your neighbor does not include robbing them, looting a store, destroying their property, or cheating them in any way. Loving my neighbor requires that I treat them with RESPECT in ALL occasions.

Each year there is a growing number of people seeking assistance with food, housing and living expenses. It seems the economies of the world are unable to provide enough jobs to properly support everyone. When will it all stop? Jesus said "For you have the poor with you always." In other words, all the charities and government programs of the world will never realize a time when the poor are no longer. While providing aide to the poor is a noble and worthy cause, raising everyone's standard of living to above the "poverty level" is seemingly not humanly possible.

We cannot educate ourselves out of our problems. We currently have the most highly educated citizenry in the history of our nation according to degree levels earned. Nearly 40% of all U.S. adults are college graduates. Academia is still belching forth its liberal stand for socialism for all, regardless of its proven failure throughout the world. Public schools have expanded programs to meet the growing demands of special needs students. Even so, education has not been able to stem the tide of societal decay. If education were the answer, crime, poverty and racism would have been all but eradicated by now. As good as education is, it will never be the cure for bad behavior.

If any of the above constructs were effective, every neighborhood and borough would be a nirvana of peace and prosperity. If any serious thinker applied real thought, peace would reign supreme throughout the land today.

Our only hope

The more man is in tune with the Infinite the less likely is to disrespect his fellow man. When people truly understand they are created in the image of God, there is a transformative power that compels them to do right regardless of circumstances. Doing the right thing should never go out of vogue. It is appropriate for all occasions, for all ages. In doing so, the commandment to "love your neighbor" takes on a whole new dimension. Cheating another person is never a consideration. Stealing never advances your cause. You know that taking an unfair advantage over others always damages your credibility. When you represent God, retaliation is not part of your modus operandi. You do not require an eye for an eye. Revenge is no longer an option. Moreover, entertaining the thought of mistreating someone is not even within your character.

The human condition brings with it a systemic problem that we cannot solve on our own. The answer is, ironically, in us. The key is discovering that the Kingdom of God is within. Our hope is in knowing who God is. It is only then that we can begin to understand others and ourselves. When we know the answer to these conditions, we are in a position to effect a permanent change for the Good. We must first know God.

CHAPTER 2

The Symbiotic Relationship Of God And Man

God's commitment to Man & Mans reliance on God

It is important that we begin to study the attributes of God and know how we relate to those attributes. As we learn what they are, they will shape our concept of who God is and acquire a working concept of who we are in God's creation.

It is not of our choosing, but of necessity that we understand the nature of being, existence, and the universal scheme of things. Since God sets the rules, it would behoove us to know what they are. Who is God? Do I really need to answer to God? What is our significance in such a vast universe? What are the implications of living in this world? What are the expectations placed upon us? What are my responsibilities?

In discovering who God is, we can make a list of attributes, and support our findings through Holy Scriptures. In the process of doing that, we can also construct a list of man's attributes, as a genuine response in knowing who God is.

Defining God and who we are at the same time allows us to keep everything in its proper perspective. The roles of God v. Man are not blurred, and must maintain their intended distinctions. Man is dependent on God and God offers man a unique relationship afforded to no other part of creation. We must first understand this relationship to fully appreciate the immensity of God's love and care for us. **We are not an afterthought of God**, or something added to creation at the last minute. God reserved the best of creation for us as us. We are the perfect compliment to God.

Action Required

As we discover these attributes of God and who we are, make a list of statements or affirmations to recite daily. These should be spoken audibly and rapidly, defining God and our relationship to God. Growth in confidence and faith is guaranteed to be transformational.

God is Atonement

There are different ways of expressing our natural condition before God. Our failings are referred to as transgressions, sin, iniquity, missing the mark, or simply the absence of faith. Transgressions are a reference to violating Gods laws. We transgress whether by accident or design. We sin as an act of rebellion, knowing what God expects yet behaving in the contrary. Man's free will gives him the option of being compliant or defiant regarding Gods commands.

God solves our problem through atonement for sin. A merciful and loving God steps in and makes amends for our wrongdoing. God rebukes the punishment that was due us. Since man has no atoning power of his own, we are 100% dependent on Gods atoning love. God's love gift became atonement because of our need.

Help us, O God of our salvation, for the glory of thy name: and deliver us, and purge away our sins, for thy name's sake.
Psalm 79:9

By mercy and truth iniquity is purged: and by the fear of the Lord men depart from evil.
Proverbs 16:6

That thou mayest remember, and be confounded, and never open thy mouth any more because of thy shame, when I am pacified toward thee for all that thou hast done, saith the Lord God.
Ezekiel 16:63

I am Atoneable

We have in our pride and ignorance, attempted to atone for our own sins. Self supposes it can atone for such transgressions through offerings of gifts. It is presumptuous to suppose that God is interested in the same things that we value. To offer gifts and sacrifices is telling of what we think about God. We suppose we know what will impress God only because the "sacrifice" we offer impresses us. We live in hope that forfeiting something we value will impress God. We expect this act of divesting ourselves of something we enjoy, will solve our problem. We desperately seek atonement for our sins, and ignorantly attempt to fix the problem on our own. "Never mind God, I've got this one." "I'll handle the small stuff and check back with you later if something I can't handle happens." The truth is, all sin problems are beyond our ability with which to deal. God's love gift of atonement always takes care of the sin problem. Anything less than God is inadequate.

You are not bothering God when you accept God's atonement in your life, you are honoring God with your love.

———⇒●∈———

We have therefore brought an oblation for the Lord, what every man hath gotten, of jewels of gold, chains, and bracelets, rings, earrings, and tablets, to make an atonement for our souls before the Lord.

Numbers 31:50

And not only so, but we also joy in God through our Lord Jesus Christ, by whom we have now received the atonement.

Romans 5:11

God is Begetter

Reading the verses below, one soon learns that to be begotten, holds a unique and holy place among God's creation. Jesus being begotten of God the Father alludes to the deity of Christ, in that the Son proceeds from the Father.

———➤●◄———

I will declare the decree: the Lord hath said unto me, Thou art my Son; this day have I begotten thee.

Psalm 2:7

And the Word was made flesh, and dwelt among us, (and we beheld his glory, the glory as of the only begotten of the Father,) full of grace and truth.

John 1:14

For God so loved the world, that he gave his only begotten Son, that whosoever believeth in him should not perish, but have everlasting life.

John 3:16

God hath fulfilled the same unto us their children, in that he hath raised up Jesus again; as it is also written in the second psalm, Thou art my Son, this day have I begotten thee.

Acts 13:33

So also Christ glorified not himself to be made an high priest; but he that said unto him, Thou art my Son, to day have I begotten thee.

Hebrews 5:5

In this was manifested the love of God toward us, because that God sent his only begotten Son into the world, that we might live through him.

1John 4:9

I am Begotten

Man, who by his very nature is begotten of God, is held in high esteem. God created man in His image. Can you think of a greater honor than to emulate Almighty God? It is most certainly the case that man too often overlooks this highest of positions among all of Gods creation. God has reserved this distinction for man and man alone.

I am begotten of God to serve a purpose that no other part of Gods creation can fulfill. I am begotten of God to experience by right of my birth, the full grace and mercy of all that God is, in me. I am begotten of God to bring Him pleasure. I am begotten of God that I might do all to the glory of God. I am begotten of God to praise God for who He is. I am begotten of God to be a messenger of Gods love. The exceptional nature of every human being is that he or she is so uniquely created, to serve a purpose that no other part of Gods creation can fulfill. This is the true meaning of being God's beloved in whom the begetter is well pleased.

⟶≫●≪⟵

Blessed be the God and Father of our Lord Jesus Christ, which according to his abundant mercy hath begotten us again unto a lively hope by the resurrection of Jesus Christ from the dead,1 Peter 1:3

Whosoever believeth that Jesus is the Christ is born of God: and every one that loveth him that begat loveth him also that is begotten of him.

1 John 5:1

God is Covenant

Because of Gods integrity, God is a covenantal God. He is a God who cannot lie. God cannot deny Himself. God conducts Himself by the same rules and the same standards all the time. All of what God does is good and reliable.

God is covenant. God has become covenant for mans sake. God's makes covenant only with a people. God as covenant demonstrates His everlasting faithfulness to mankind.

The Lord our God made a covenant with us in Horeb.
Deuteronomy 5:2

And the covenant that I have made with you ye shall not forget; neither shall ye fear other gods.
2 Kings 17:38

Therefore the word of the Lord came to Jeremiah from the Lord, saying, Thus saith the Lord, the God of Israel; I made a covenant with your fathers in the day that I brought them forth out of the land of Egypt, out of the house of bondmen, saying,
Jeremiah 34:12-13

And I prayed unto the Lord my God, and made my confession, and said, O Lord, the great and dreadful God, keeping the covenant and mercy to them that love him, and to them that keep his commandments;
Daniel 9:4

Ye are the children of the prophets, and of the covenant which God made with our fathers, saying unto Abraham, And in thy seed shall all the kindreds of the earth be blessed.
Acts 3:25

I am Covenantal

Among all the covenants in the Bible, the final most profound is the blood covenant. God's fulfillment of this covenant is the promise of salvation. God made good on his word to provide a sacrifice for sin.

I am covenantal with God. My salvation is as secure as God is true to His word. God's very nature is covenant, an unchanging attribute of God. Because I am covenantal, I have entered into an everlasting agreement with God concerning salvation.

———⇒>●<⇐———

And Moses took the blood, and sprinkled it on the people, and said, Behold the blood of the covenant, which the Lord hath made with you concerning all these words.
Exodus 24:8

And he caused all that were present in Jerusalem and Benjamin to stand to it. And the inhabitants of Jerusalem did according to the covenant of God, the God of their fathers.
2 Chronicles 34:32

Brethren, I speak after the manner of men; Though it be but a man's covenant, yet if it be confirmed, no man disannulleth, or addeth thereto.
Galatians 3:15

Saying, This is the blood of the testament which God hath enjoined unto you.
Hebrews 9:20

Now the God of peace, that brought again from the dead our Lord Jesus, that great shepherd of the sheep, through the blood of the everlasting covenant,
Hebrews 13:20

God is Fulfillment

All of Gods promises are yes and amen, meaning they are absolute and complete. There is never anything left undone or partially completed with God. God is fulfillment, is a statement of absoluteness. There is nothing more that must be done.

———<>●<———

And the Lord hath performed his word that he spake,
1 Kings 8:20a

And he said, Blessed be the Lord God of Israel, who hath with his hands fulfilled that which he spake with his mouth to my father David, saying,
2 Chronicles 6:4

The Lord therefore hath performed his word that he hath spoken: for I am risen up in the room of David my father, and am set on the throne of Israel, as the Lord promised, and have built the house for the name of the Lord God of Israel.
2 Chronicles 6:10

But those things, which God before had shewed by the mouth of all his prophets, that Christ should suffer, he hath so fulfilled.
Acts 3:18

God hath fulfilled the same unto us their children, in that he hath raised up Jesus again; as it is also written in the second psalm, Thou art my Son, this day have I begotten thee.
Acts 13:33

And the scripture was fulfilled which saith, Abraham believed God, and it was imputed unto him for righteousness: and he was called the Friend of God.
James 2:23

I am Fulfilled

When we bring our petitions before the Lord it should be with the expectation of being fulfilled. If there seems to be anything lacking, it is incumbent on us to take stock in what we are asking. Are we even taking the proper amount of time to ask? When we do come before the Lord, are we petitioning for a holy cause or merely interested in satisfying selfish desires?

God is certainly willing and able to fulfill our hearts desire. I am fulfilled knowing that Gods best is always available to me.

I am fulfilled because the kingdom of God is at hand. There is no greater gift or blessing than what God has given me in Jesus Christ. I am fulfilled because all that the kingdom of God has to offer is afforded to me.

I am fulfilled because the truth of Gods word is fulfilled. I cannot improve on Gods word; I can only proclaim Gods word as true, complete, and everlasting.

We will rejoice in thy salvation, and in the name of our God we will set up our banners: the Lord fulfil all thy petitions.
Psalm 20:5

And saying, The time is fulfilled, and the kingdom of God is at hand: repent ye, and believe the gospel.
Mark 1:15

Whereof I am made a minister, according to the dispensation of God which is given to me for you, to fulfil the word of God;
Colossians 1:25

God is Government

God is government. God exemplifies what it means to be a Holy, righteous, and just ruler. Wonderful counselor alludes to the wisest of all sages, even that of King Solomon. The title Mighty God means there will never be a time when Gods power fades. There will never be a time when God does not exist. God himself is the epitome of peace, the source of all peace.

While we have governments and hierarchies of governments on earth, the highest of which are still subject to the governing rule of God. God is government. God oversees the nations of the world. God allows us to campaign and debate issues. God gives each man the power and position he enjoys. No ruler is set in office but what God has appointed them. God's authority being ultimate is also final. It would be presumptuous to suppose that all that is accomplished through government happens independent from the hand of God. Governmental authority is an extension of Gods rule over man.

For unto us a child is born, unto us a son is given: and the government shall be upon his shoulder: and his name shall be called Wonderful, Counsellor, The mighty God, The everlasting Father, The Prince of Peace.

Isaiah 9:6

Let every soul be subject unto the higher powers. For there is no power but of God: the powers that be are ordained of God.

Romans 13:1

I am Governable

Man was made in the image of God. As such, man is more complex than the animals of this world. God made man a little lower than the angels. God also made man to govern and to be governed. We are certainly above the social plane of animals, and need a command a greater sense of order and discipline. Man is governable, to better accomplish the will of God the Father.

Man's order is not to supersede or supplant Gods ways, but mirror the kingdom of God. We are confident that every ordinance of God has purpose, but what about the ordinances of man? It is also incumbent upon us to follow the laws of the land. In doing so, we are honoring God. Violating any statute design to prevent one individual from having an unfair advantage over another is also violating Gods law "love your neighbor as yourself."

No doubt, governments are composed of individuals who are posturing for position and power. They seek recognition and praise. Whether they are intentional or not, rulers have certain responsibility toward those they govern. Ideally they are there for the good of the people. Ultimately, they are accountable to God for how they performed.

Submit yourselves to every ordinance of man for the Lord's sake: whether it be to the king, as supreme;
1 Peter 2:13

Obey them that have the rule over you, and submit yourselves: for they watch for your souls, as they that must give account, that they may do it with joy, and not with grief: for that is unprofitable for you.
Hebrews 13:17

God is Guidance

Because no one is born with a life's roadmap, God is prepared to guide us individually each step of the way. Because there are multiple paths for us to choose, we need to determine which path leads to the best possible outcome. When we proceed on our own volition, we risk heartache and disappointment. However, one bad choice needn't doom us to failure. God is always there to help us recover, but more importantly, God is guidance who helps us avoid the pitfalls. God is guidance because He knows us and our capabilities.

———————

Thou in thy mercy hast led forth the people which thou hast redeemed: thou hast guided them in thy strength unto thy holy habitation.
Exodus 15:13

The meek will he guide in judgment: and the meek will he teach his way.
Psalm 25:9

For this God is our God for ever and ever: he will be our guide even unto death.
Psalm 48:14

And the Lord shall guide thee continually, and satisfy thy soul in drought, and make fat thy bones: and thou shalt be like a watered garden, and like a spring of water, whose waters fail not.
Isaiah 58:11

I am Guided

If God likens man to sheep it is to illustrate that we have a need for shepherding. From our perspective, we are intelligent, skilled in building, organizing and executing plans. Man is not capable of gazing into the future and taking note of all the obstacles that could be avoided. Even the most adept and learned of us are ill equipped to navigate through life's trials and tribulations. I am guided because I am not designed to weigh endless possibilities. This is God's job and His good pleasure to do so. Mine is to be sensitive to the direction He is leading me.

Any time we take the reigns on our own, it is an affront to God. We are telling God Almighty we do not need Him. There is no glory in suffering for our bad decisions. There is no shame in succeeding, because God guided us.

But made his own people to go forth like sheep, and guided them in the wilderness like a flock.

Psalm 78:52

A good man sheweth favour, and lendeth: he will guide his affairs with discretion.

Psalm 112:5

And he said, How can I, except some man should guide me? And he desired Philip that he would come up and sit with him.

Acts 8:31

God is the Head of the church

If you needed to know what thing someone placed the highest value on was, you would take note of what they devoted the most time and attention to. You could know for sure of its value, by how much of themselves they gave to that particular thing. And so it is with God. When it came to the redemption of man, God in Jesus gave all that He had, His body and blood. This is the birthright of the church. The salvation of mans soul was bought with a price. What was purchased with Jesus blood belongs to Jesus. Jesus, through the Holy Spirit instituted the church. No man can lay claim to ownership or oversight of the church. Christ alone is the head of the Christian Church.

———⟫●⟪———

Take heed therefore unto yourselves, and to all the flock, over the which the Holy Ghost hath made you overseers, to feed the church of God, which he hath purchased with his own blood.
Acts 20:28

Give none offence, neither to the Jews, nor to the Gentiles, nor to the church of God:
1 Corinthians 10:32

And hath put all things under his feet, and gave him to be the head over all things to the church,
Ephesians 1:22

For the husband is the head of the wife, even as Christ is the head of the church: and he is the saviour of the body.
Ephesians 5:23

And he is the head of the body, the church: who is the beginning, the firstborn from the dead; that in all things he might have the preeminence.
Colossians 1:18

I am the Body of the church

We, as members, are the body of Christ.
Christ is the head of the body.
We are one of many members comprising the body.
Christ is the head of the Church.

So we, being many, are one body in Christ, and every one members one of another.
Romans 12:5

For as the body is one, and hath many members, and all the members of that one body, being many, are one body: so also is Christ. For by one Spirit are we all baptized into one body, whether we be Jews or Gentiles, whether we be bond or free; and have been all made to drink into one Spirit. For the body is not one member, but many.
1 Corinthians 12:12-14

Now ye are the body of Christ, and members in particular.
1 Corinthians 12:27

Who now rejoice in my sufferings for you, and fill up that which is behind of the afflictions of Christ in my flesh for his body's sake, which is the church:
Colossians 1:24

God is Judge

One of the functions of our righteous God is that of judge. God judges man with regard to sin and works. The wicked are judged and receive their corresponding consequences. God also judges or affects mans path in life. At Gods discretion, He curtails the action of one and blesses or advances the cause of another. God, who judges all, must also judge those who have placed their faith in Jesus Christ. Theirs is a judgment of rewards.

God judgeth the righteous, and God is angry with the wicked every day.
Psalm 7:11

And the heavens shall declare his righteousness: for God is judge himself. Selah.
Psalm 50:6

So that a man shall say, Verily there is a reward for the righteous: verily he is a God that judgeth in the earth.
Psalm 58:11

But God is the judge: he putteth down one, and setteth up another.
Psalm 75:7

In the day when God shall judge the secrets of men by Jesus Christ according to my gospel.
Romans 2:16

Marriage is honourable in all, and the bed undefiled: but whoremongers and adulterers God will judge.
Hebrews 13:4

I am Judged

Judgment by God is always fair and balanced. Everyone plays by the same set of rules. The standard that we hold others to is the same standard God requires of us. This can serve as both a warning to the unjust and an encouragement to the just. There is no secret concerning God's expectations for man. He has shown you, *"O man, what is good; And what does the Lord require of you But to do justly, To love mercy, And to walk humbly with your God?" Micah 6:8*. God in His righteousness ensures all that is done in the name of judgment, is in keeping with His love and mercy. No other is qualified or permitted to judge man. God's character only allows for righteous judgment. God's judgment is just.

For with what judgment you judge, you will be judged; and with the measure you use, it will be measured back to you.
Matthew 7:2

And now I stand and am judged for the hope of the promise made by God to our fathers.
Acts 26:6

For I know of nothing against myself, yet I am not justified by this; but He who judges me is the Lord.
1 Corinthians 4:4

So speak and so do as those who will be judged by the law of liberty.
James 2:12

God is Justifying

Justification is for the righteous. This is not to say a sinless soul, but one who has been declared blameless. The prosecutor has levied legitimate charges. However, the verdict rendered is in favor of the accused because of Jesus. Even Jesus was "justified in the spirit" or vindicated from any accusations of improprieties.

Then hear thou in heaven, and do, and judge thy servants, condemning the wicked, to bring his way upon his head; and justifying the righteous, to give him according to his righteousness.
1 Kings 8:32

Then hear thou from heaven, and do, and judge thy servants, by requiting the wicked, by recompensing his way upon his own head; and by justifying the righteous, by giving him according to his righteousness.
2 Chronicles 6:23

In the Lord shall all the seed of Israel be justified, and shall glory.
Isaiah 45:25

And without controversy great is the mystery of godliness: God was manifest in the flesh, justified in the Spirit, seen of angels, preached unto the Gentiles, believed on in the world, received up into glory.
1 Timothy 3:16

I am Justified

It is never enough just to know the law of God. It is incumbent upon us to be doers of the law. Man is justified by faith in Christ, and the evidence of that justifying faith is good works. Faith and good works go hand in hand. That is why James makes the claim that "man is justified by works." Mans sees the outward manifestation of faith which is the justification of works. God knows the heart of man, who is in truth, justified by faith.

<hr />

(For not the hearers of the law are just before God, but the doers of the law shall be justified.
Romans 2:13

Therefore we conclude that a man is justified by faith without the deeds of the law.
Romans 3:28

Therefore being justified by faith, we have peace with God through our Lord Jesus Christ:
Romans 5:1

And such were some of you: but ye are washed, but ye are sanctified, but ye are justified in the name of the Lord Jesus, and by the Spirit of our God.
1 Corinthians 6:11

But that no man is justified by the law in the sight of God, it is evident: for, The just shall live by faith.
Galatians 3:11

Ye see then how that by works a man is justified, and not by faith only.
James 2:24

God is Liberty

There is liberty in the being of God because love cannot be confounded. God's love is a perfect love and knows no bounds. God's love is at liberty to affect whosoever, which is also a testament to God's unconditional love. It is the very spirit of the Lord that grants us liberty.

⟫●⟪

The Spirit of the Lord God is upon me; because the Lord hath anointed me to preach good tidings unto the meek; he hath sent me to bind up the brokenhearted, to proclaim liberty to the captives, and the opening of the prison to them that are bound;
Isaiah 61:1

The Spirit of the Lord is upon me, because he hath anointed me to preach the gospel to the poor; he hath sent me to heal the brokenhearted, to preach deliverance to the captives, and recovering of sight to the blind, to set at liberty them that are bruised,
Luke 4:18

Therefore thus saith the Lord; Ye have not hearkened unto me, in proclaiming liberty, every one to his brother, and every man to his neighbour: behold, I proclaim a liberty for you, saith the Lord, to the sword, to the pestilence, and to the famine; and I will make you to be removed into all the kingdoms of the earth.
Jeremiah 34:17

Now the Lord is that Spirit: and where the Spirit of the Lord is, there is liberty.
2 Corinthians 3:17

I am Liberated

The liberty that man receives from God gives us the latitude to live as we please under canopy of God's laws. We need to recognize this same inalienable right in others. We are to extend liberty to all. No man has the right to encumber the liberty of another. This capsulizes what it means to love your neighbor. Never allow the exercising of your liberties to encroach on the liberties of others.

And ye were now turned, and had done right in my sight, in proclaiming liberty every man to his neighbour; and ye had made a covenant before me in the house which is called by my name:
Jeremiah 34:15

Because the creature itself also shall be delivered from the bondage of corruption into the glorious liberty of the children of God.
Romans 8:21

For, brethren, ye have been called unto liberty; only use not liberty for an occasion to the flesh, but by love serve one another.
Galatians 5:13

For so is the will of God, that with well doing ye may put to silence the ignorance of foolish men: As free, and not using your liberty for a cloke of maliciousness, but as the servants of God.
1 Peter 2:15-16

God is Maintainer

When we are living for a right cause, God enables us to stay on track or maintain the right course of action. This takes on the form of God maintaining our sustenance, our life purpose, championing the cause of the afflicted and ensuring justice for the poor.

———◈———

And let these my words, wherewith I have made supplication before the Lord, be nigh unto the Lord our God day and night, that he maintain the cause of his servant, and the cause of his people Israel at all times, as the matter shall require:
1 Kings 8:59

The Lord is the portion of mine inheritance and of my cup: thou maintainest my lot.
Psalm 16:5

I know that the Lord will maintain the cause of the afflicted, and the right of the poor.
Psalm 140:12

I am Maintainable

Those who believe in God are expected to demonstrate good works. It is not a matter of doing works to impress God. The Lord admonishes us to do this for our own good. It is profitable for man to perform good works. There is the obvious benefit for the good of others; there is reciprocal effect for good on self.

———∞———

This is a faithful saying, and these things I will that thou affirm constantly, that they which have believed in God might be careful to maintain good works. These things are good and profitable unto men.
Titus 3:8

God is Ordainer

God as Ordainer assigns man tasks that can only be explained by His intimate knowledge of us. Being created in God's image automatically gives us a one-upmanship over all other creation. Not only that, God makes man a living soul, an individual with a uniquely assigned set of skills, abilities and temperament. God alone knows how we can best use those attributes, because we are His design.

Even from our infancy God has ordained our strength of qualities and provided opportunities to use them. It is incumbent on us to discover those qualities and purpose to use them for good.

With regard to man, there are no random events. Wisdom is in understanding that we are designed for a purpose, and what has been ordained of God will be fulfilled. Man should ultimately be a perfect expression of life.

———————

Out of the mouth of babes and sucklings hast thou ordained strength because of thine enemies, that thou mightest still the enemy and the avenger. When I consider thy heavens, the work of thy fingers, the moon and the stars, which thou hast ordained;
Psalm 8:2-3

And he commanded us to preach unto the people, and to testify that it is he which was ordained of God to be the Judge of quick and dead.
Acts 10:42

But we speak the wisdom of God in a mystery, even the hidden wisdom, which God ordained before the world unto our glory:
1 Corinthians 2:7

I am Ordained

Life purpose in not something to be manufactured by teachers, counselors, or clergy. Life purpose is ordained of God. Life is a process of demonstrating that purpose. I am ordained with an assigned role in this world that no one else can fulfill.

Being made in the image of God means we are ordained to live a certain life: one whose hallmark is righteousness. It is not enough that we should live a life of pleasing God on earth, we have the assurance of a resurrected life which is eternal with God the father.

I am ordained of God to live my life through the work of His Church. Christ gave Himself for the church, consequently our greatest influence and holiest of contributions is through the church.

———————

Before I formed thee in the belly I knew thee; and before thou camest forth out of the womb I sanctified thee, and I ordained thee a prophet unto the nations.

Jeremiah 1:5

Because he hath appointed a day, in the which he will judge the world in righteousness by that man whom he hath ordained; whereof he hath given assurance unto all men, in that he hath raised him from the dead.

Acts 17:31

But as God hath distributed to every man, as the Lord hath called every one, so let him walk. And so ordain I in all churches.

1 Corinthians 7:17

God is the Potter

The potter forms the clay according to his idea of what the clay should be. The potter has influence over the clay. Whatever idea the potter has will be realized in the clay. The potter in this case, is the father figure.

The father has influence over the child. He is charged with forming this young life into something that is honorable and purposeful. The father uses his discretion toward providing the child's needs. In His wisdom, he knows what is needed, when it is needed and to what extent it is needed. The father is there to provide guidance as long as the child needs it.

God works that same way in the lives of men. God influences our lives along the way to mold us into something honorable and useful: a creation that brings praise to Him, a creation that reflects His Glory. This illustrates how God both deals with individuals and nations.

———————

But now, O Lord, thou art our father; we are the clay, and thou our potter; and we all are the work of thy hand.

Isaiah 64:8

O house of Israel, cannot I do with you as this potter? saith the Lord. Behold, as the clay is in the potter's hand, so are ye in mine hand, O house of Israel.

eremiah 18:6

The precious sons of Zion, comparable to fine gold, how are they esteemed as earthen pitchers, the work of the hands of the potter!

Lamentations 4:2

I am the Clay

Clay is a substance without form. This substance, in the hands of a skilled potter can take on many forms. The clay itself has no concept of what it might become. It's future is contingent on the mind of the potter. The clay does not dictate to the potter. The clay simply makes itself available to the potter.

The child looks to the father for security, and protection and provision. The child knows that he has needs, but can't always determine or predict what they may be. The father has the best vantage point to know the needs of the child. The father does not seek advise from the child. The child does not have the life experience to make wise decisions. In his ignorance, he may even make demands of the father or have temper tantrums. It is the father's duty to always provide what is best for the child, regardless of acting out.

God, our loving father, expresses his watch-care and guidance in much the same way. Our creator knows what is best for us. God has insight into our lives than we know nothing of. Our responsibility is to subject our lives to him, knowing He always has our best interest at hand. Our choice is in whether we allow God to make us a vessel of honor, or insist on opposing Him and becoming a vessel of dishonor.

Hath not the potter power over the clay, of the same lump to make one vessel unto honour, and another unto dishonour?
Romans 9:21

God is Praised

Praise is Gods just do from His creation. Worthy means God, and God alone is to be praised.

Protection from the Lord is an outgrowth of our praise to Him.

Praising any thing or any other entity is idolatry. Nothing is to be revered above God. No other thing that exists is equal to God.

Since praise is worship reserved for the almighty, there is no quantity too great or too frequent for this display of devotion. God is to be praised throughout our day. There is no limit to God's greatness; there is no limit to His praise.

I will call on the Lord, who is worthy to be praised: so shall I be saved from mine enemies.

2 Samuel 22:4

For great is the Lord, and greatly to be praised: he also is to be feared above all gods.

1 Chronicles 16:25

From the rising of the sun unto the going down of the same the Lord's name is to be praised.

Psalm 113:3

Great is the Lord, and greatly to be praised; and his greatness is unsearchable.

Psalm 145:3

I am Praising

We are to praise God in all of His dwelling places.

We are to praise God for our knowing of Him: all that is within our consciousness of Him. We are to praise God for His mighty works. We praise God when He draws nigh unto us.

Praising God is not a one-way street; it produces joy in our lives.

Praising God touches the hearts of other people, which in turn draws more men to God.

Praise ye the Lord. Praise God in his sanctuary: praise him in the firmament of his power.

Psalm 150:1

And the shepherds returned, glorifying and praising God for all the things that they had heard and seen, as it was told unto them.

Luke 2:20

And when he was come nigh, even now at the descent of the mount of Olives, the whole multitude of the disciples began to rejoice and praise God with a loud voice for all the mighty works that they had seen;

Luke 19:37

And they worshipped him, and returned to Jerusalem with great joy: And were continually in the temple, praising and blessing God. Amen.

Luke 24:52-53

Praising God, and having favour with all the people. And the Lord added to the church daily such as should be saved.

Acts 2:47

God is Revelation

God is selective in revealing His plan to mankind. God chooses the person and place for a specific purpose. God's revelation to Samuel was for the benefit of a nation.

God gives the revelation of truth to individuals that we may know Him. "...The Son of God is come, and hath given us an understanding, that we may know him that is true..." 1 John 5:20

It is God's revelation through the ages that has communicated His loving grace to mankind.

———————

And the child Samuel ministered unto the Lord before Eli. And the word of the Lord was precious in those days; there was no open vision.

Samuel 3:1

That the God of our Lord Jesus Christ, the Father of glory, may give unto you the spirit of wisdom and revelation in the knowledge of him:

Ephesians 1:17

Wherefore gird up the loins of your mind, be sober, and hope to the end for the grace that is to be brought unto you at the revelation of Jesus Christ;

1 Peter 1:13

I am Revelational

As a believer in the Almighty, His gift of salvation is revealed to all who come to Him. Jesus' revelation before God the Father confirms man as blameless.

Our knowledge and abilities is nothing that we should boast of. They are not a product of our own doing. They are the manifestations of the Lords revelations in our lives.

———————

Even as the testimony of Christ was confirmed in you: So that ye come behind in no gift; waiting for the coming of our Lord Jesus Christ: Who shall also confirm you unto the end, that ye may be blameless in the day of our Lord Jesus Christ.
1 Corinthians 1:6-8

It is not expedient for me doubtless to glory. I will come to visions and revelations of the Lord.
2 Corinthians 12:1

For I neither received it of man, neither was I taught it, but by the revelation of Jesus Christ.
Galatians 1:12

That the God of our Lord Jesus Christ, the Father of glory, may give unto you the spirit of wisdom and revelation in the knowledge of him:
Ephesians 1:17

God is Satisfaction

God's satisfaction is living through mankind.

God is pleased to satisfy the needs of man, even in providing him with the "bread of heaven" which is the best God has to offer.

God is so devoted to caring for man that He ensures that our very being (soul) realizes satisfaction in the face of adversity. As we face circumstances that may cause others into panic, our satisfaction is in knowing all the provision we need now, or will ever need, are available.

With long life will I satisfy him, and shew him my salvation.
Psalm 91:16

The people asked, and he brought quails, and satisfied them with the bread of heaven.
Psalm 105:40

And the Lord shall guide thee continually, and satisfy thy soul in drought, and make fat thy bones: and thou shalt be like a watered garden, and like a spring of water, whose waters fail not.
Isaiah 58:11

I am Satisfied

My satisfaction is in knowing that God is a righteous God. Mine is to realize life is not my own, but one that is given to me by God. The influence of God in my life yields satisfaction. I am confident that all is well. As I grow closer to God, I am awakened to my mirroring the likeness of God.

Whatever you hunger for, God is willing and able to satisfy. God is not in the business of temporary fixes or band-aiding a problem. His affect in my life is an everlasting effect.

There is satisfaction to be gained from labor. Frivolity in place of work; robs me of material gain and denies me of valuable life lessons.

———◄►◄———

As for me, I will behold thy face in righteousness: I shall be satisfied, when I awake, with thy likeness.

Psalm 17:15

The meek shall eat and be satisfied: they shall praise the Lord that seek him: your heart shall live for ever.

Psalm 22:26

Blessed is the man whom thou choosest, and causest to approach unto thee, that he may dwell in thy courts: we shall be satisfied with the goodness of thy house, even of thy holy temple.

Psalm 65:4

He that tilleth his land shall be satisfied with bread: but he that followeth vain persons is void of understanding.

Proverbs 12:11

A man shall be satisfied with good by the fruit of his mouth: and the recompence of a man's hands shall be rendered unto him.

Proverbs 12:14

God is Thankfulness

Jesus gave thanks to God the Father for provision. Jesus' response was not a simple "thank you" after being handed a gift. It was a thank you to God for who He is. Jesus thanked God the Father knowing the character of God includes His provision for mankind. It was not a question of God being able, or God being willing. We put these limitations on God to excuse the lack of His intervention in our lives. Even a child knows to say thank you when receiving a gift. The lesson Jesus is teaching us is to thank God at all times. Thank God for the gifts He is ready to give you now. Thank God for all futures gifts He has planned for you.

———————

And he took the seven loaves and the fishes, and gave thanks, and brake them, and gave to his disciples, and the disciples to the multitude.

Matthew 15:36

And he took the cup, and when he had given thanks, he gave it to them: and they all drank of it.

Mark 14:23

And he took bread, and gave thanks, and brake it, and gave unto them, saying, This is my body which is given for you: this do in remembrance of me.

Luke 22:19

Saying, Amen: Blessing, and glory, and wisdom, and thanksgiving, and honour, and power, and might, be unto our God for ever and ever. Amen.

Revelation 7:12

I am Thanksgiving

Of the many things deserving of our thanks to God are His holy name, righteousness, goodness, wonderful works, mercy, and righteous judgments. I am thanksgiving in prayer, as I bring my requests before the Lord.

———————

Sing unto the Lord, O ye saints of his, and give thanks at the remembrance of his holiness.
Psalm 30:4

Rejoice in the Lord, ye righteous; and give thanks at the remembrance of his holiness.
Psalm 97:12

Oh that men would praise the Lord for his goodness, and for his wonderful works to the children of men!
Psalm 107:8

O give thanks unto the Lord; for he is good: because his mercy endureth for ever.
Psalm 118:1

At midnight I will rise to give thanks unto thee because of thy righteous judgments.
Psalm 119:62

Be careful for nothing; but in every thing by prayer and supplication with thanksgiving let your requests be made known unto God.
Philippians 4:6

Continue in prayer, and watch in the same with thanksgiving;
Colossians 4:2

CHAPTER 3

The Reflection of God

Whenever practicable, a rule of grammar is used to identify each heading. Because God is the Alpha and Omega, the progenitor of all that exist, the noun part of speech is used to identify the attributes of God. Because man is not just a creation of God, but also a likeness of God, he is referred to in the adjective form.

If we are to emulate the life of Christ, we need to know what those attributes are. To describe who God is and work to incorporate those qualities: is exactly what it means to be a follower of Christ. Many have learned to parrot religious jargon and are the no better off for it. Are you a practicing Christian or just someone who has learned to regurgitate religious dogma?

As you study attributes of God, you will need to spend more time reflecting on what we have in common. Doing this may bring up concerns of being presumptuous, but it is needful if we are to gain a healthy understanding of God and ourselves.

It is important to meditate on each quality. To glibly read through is to say, "God you're not that important." Just as you would not want to deny God who He is, you should not deny who you are: created in the image of God.

But whoever denies Me before men, him I will also deny before My Father who is in heaven.

Matthew 10:33

God is Abundance

God is an expression of Infinite abundance. God is the unfailing abundant supply of the Universe, who always works through a law of abundance. God created me in order that He might act and live through me. God created me according to His image of abundance. God's Holy Spirit is forever communicating ideas of divine abundance through me. God's Spirit takes note of my consciousness and forms an experience relating to my concept of abundance.

The reality of Christ within is a truth for the ages: that all may be abundantly supplied with every good thing. The mind of Christ in me develops a greater consciousness of abundance each day. The true nature of God within me is forever thinking thoughts of Abundance.

The Lord will lift me up to the High Road of abundant prosperity. The more personal I am in my relationship with the true Source of wealth, the more I will realize abundance in my life.

I place my faith in the principle of Abundance that emanates from God almighty.

Just as a wise philosopher enriches his mind abundantly in a general knowledge of things, so should man embrace the abundance of God.

———————

The thief cometh not, but for to steal, and to kill, and to destroy: I am come that they might have life, and that they might have it more abundantly.

John 10:10

I am Abundant

Abundance is the out-picturing of God's plan for my life.

I have an inheritance from an abundant God. I accept my God given inheritance of abundance and good. I identify myself with the all-sufficient Creator, who knows only abundance. I am totally free of any notions of self-sufficiency and confident that God will always appear as the abundant all-sufficiency in my life and affairs.

I believe that God the Father is the Source of all Abundance and that I am the product of God's limitless wealth. I am conscious of the Holy Spirit guiding me to all Abundance. I acknowledge the Spirit of God as the conduit of my abundance. I am a living testament to Christ's abundant Salvation. I am mindful the nature of God's abundance lives within me. I take comfort in knowing that the activity of Divine Abundance is eternally operating in my life.

Daily, I seek to replace ideas of lack with ideas of abundance. I think of myself as already living in the abundant manner that God desires for me. The joy of my vision is realized, as I experience the abundance of the Holy Spirit in my life and affairs.

My Consciousness is forever growing and expressing God's abundance in my life.

—————>●<—————

Now unto him that is able to do exceeding abundantly above all that we ask or think, according to the power that worketh in us, Unto him be glory in the church by Christ Jesus throughout all ages, world without end. Amen.

Ephesians 3:20-21

God is Almightiness

When God revealed himself to Abram, He emphasized His quality of Almightiness. This was significant in that God was preparing to do a special work in Abram's life. God's perfect plan was contingent on Abram's understanding that God Himself would perform a mighty work, not Abram. Even so, Abram took matters into his own hands by "helping" God fulfill his promise of being the father of many nations.

One of the many descriptions of the promised messiah is "Mighty God." The Christ is mighty because God the Father is Mighty as the One and true Deity of all Creation.

Man will be exalted in time, according to the will and good pleasure of God. It is only by God and through God that man is exalted. We are not to exalt ourselves, but humble ourselves before God. It is only then, that we can be exalted by the almighty.

And when Abram was ninety years old and nine, the Lord appeared to Abram, and said unto him, I am the Almighty God; walk before me, and be thou perfect.

Genesis 17:1

For unto us a child is born, unto us a son is given: and the government shall be upon his shoulder: and his name shall be called Wonderful, Counsellor, The mighty God, The everlasting Father, The Prince of Peace.

Isaiah 9:6

Humble yourselves therefore under the mighty hand of God, that he may exalt you in due time:

1 Peter 5:6

I believe in God the Father, Almighty, Maker of heaven and earth:

Apostles Creed

I am Mighty

The expression "mighty man of valor" is used 7 times in scripture. It was Shakespeare who gave us the expression "discretion is the better part of valor." Whenever God refers to an individual as being a mighty man of valor; that is a compliment indeed. Valor suggests bravery, courage, daring and heroism. Being mighty in Biblical parlance is in reference to an individual's words, deeds, knowledge of Holy Scripture and eloquence. These are qualities that anyone can acquire, and not limited to an exclusive few. Being mighty in general, is demonstrating the power of God in your life. What qualities of God do people see in your life?

And the angel of the Lord appeared unto him, and said unto him, The Lord is with thee, thou mighty man of valour.

Judges 6:12

And Moses was learned in all the wisdom of the Egyptians, and was mighty in words and in deeds.

Acts 7:22

And a certain Jew named Apollos, born at Alexandria, an eloquent man, and mighty in the scriptures, came to Ephesus.

Acts 18:24

Truly the signs of an apostle were wrought among you in all patience, in signs, and wonders, and mighty deeds.

2 Corinthians 12:12

God is Beauty

It is said that beauty is in the eyes of the beholder. All that we see in God's creation reflects the beauty of God. When we read in Psalm 19:1 "The heavens declare the glory of God; And the firmament shows His handiwork" it is a picture of the vastness and beauty of God's creation. There is beauty in everything God creates. God is the personification of beauty. God is the source of all beauty.

Beauty is the balanced portrayal of Life, Truth, and Love. In any true work of art, you will view these three aspects of beauty.

One thing have I desired of the Lord, that will I seek after; that I may dwell in the house of the Lord all the days of my life, to behold the beauty of the Lord, and to enquire in his temple.

Psalm 27:4

And let the beauty of the Lord our God be upon us: and establish thou the work of our hands upon us; yea, the work of our hands establish thou it.

Psalm 90:17

I am Beautiful

Of all God's creation he chose one thing and one thing alone to represent His beauty. Man has the highest honor to be made in the image of God. This is no accident. In the six days of creation He literally reserved the best for last. We are Gods crowning achievement. We are "fearfully and wonderfully made." We are the objects of Gods love. We are the recipients of His beauty. I am beautiful because God made me.

There is beauty in those who bring peace and glad tidings to man. There is beauty in those who preach the good news of salvation.

There should be beauty to adorn, all great and important undertakings.

The carpenter stretcheth out his rule; he marketh it out with a line; he fitteth it with planes, and he marketh it out with the compass, and maketh it after the figure of a man, according to the beauty of a man; that it may remain in the house.

Isaiah 44:13

How beautiful upon the mountains are the feet of him that bringeth good tidings, that publisheth peace; that bringeth good tidings of good, that publisheth salvation; that saith unto Zion, Thy God reigneth!

Isaiah 52:7

And how shall they preach, except they be sent? as it is written, How beautiful are the feet of them that preach the gospel of peace, and bring glad tidings of good things!

Romans 10:15

God is Christ

God became flesh and dwelt among us. This was the Christ, the promised messiah, Jesus. He "made himself of no reputation, and took upon him the form of a servant, and was made in the likeness of men:" (Philippians 2:7) Jesus being the Christ was truly "God with us." Jesus at the right hand of the Father is equal in glory and majesty composing the trinity.

———

Therefore let all the house of Israel know assuredly, that God hath made the same Jesus, whom ye have crucified, both Lord and Christ.
Acts 2:36

The word which God sent unto the children of Israel, preaching peace by Jesus Christ: (he is Lord of all:)
Acts 10:36

He first findeth his own brother Simon, and saith unto him, We have found the Messias, which is, being interpreted, the Christ.
John 1:41

And without controversy great is the mystery of godliness: God was manifest in the flesh, justified in the Spirit, seen of angels, preached unto the Gentiles, believed on in the world, received up into glory.
1 Timothy 3:16

I am Christ-like

I am Christ-like in as much as I reflect His God given attributes. They reveal the image of God that I am. I am Christ-like in discovering and living God's truth. I am Christ-like knowing the mind of Christ. I am Christ-like in making Him my rule of life. I am Christ-like as the Holy Spirit bears witness. I am Christ-like as an ambassador of God's love. I am Christ-like as an everlasting influence for good. Christ-likeness is my legacy. Nothing can separate "me" from the love of God, which is in Christ Jesus "my" Lord.

⟫●⟪

Now the God of patience and consolation grant you to be likeminded one toward another according to Christ Jesus:
Romans 15:5

Now we command you, brethren, in the name of our Lord Jesus Christ, that ye withdraw yourselves from every brother that walketh disorderly, and not after the tradition which he received of us.
2 Thessalonians 3:6

God is Commitment

Commitment is Gods very nature. He is committed to truth, love, and provision for mankind. Gods commitment to man has no loopholes, or escape clause. God is so committed to reconciling Himself to mankind this plan was in place before creation. It was a contingency made before the "fall of man." We are not an afterthought in the mind of God. We are first and foremost in the mind of God. God reserved breathing the breath of life into man on the sixth day of creation. God saved the best of his creation for last: mankind. Only man is said to have the distinction of being created in the "image" of God. We have the honor of receiving God's highest compliment. Mankind has the very image of God stamped on his soul.

———————

To wit, that God was in Christ, reconciling the world unto himself, not imputing their trespasses unto them; and hath committed unto us the word of reconciliation.
2 Corinthians 5:19

In hope of eternal life, which God, that cannot lie, promised before the world began; But hath in due times manifested his word through preaching, which is committed unto me according to the commandment of God our Saviour;
Titus 1:2-3

I am Committed

Being committed to God follows the form of cause. We are committed to God for a purpose: The purpose of praise and worship or the purpose of prosperity, health, creative expression and love. Being committed to God reserves a special place in ones heart that no other person of entity can satisfy. We are 100% convinced that God and God alone can meet our immediate needs or any future needs.

We are implicitly committed to the oracles of God. There is not deceit, subterfuge or anything less than honorable in God's messages to us. The truth of God's word is to be trusted above all.

Being committed to God means trusting fully in the gospel of Christ. There is no equivalent, there is no substitute for the gospel. Knowing that, our faith is well founded in the truth of His written word. His Holy Spirit best guides our spirit.

God in turn honors our commitment to Him with entrusting us to communicate this same message of Gods love to fellow man.

———⟫●⟪———

I would seek unto God, and unto God would I commit my cause:
Job 5:8

Much every way: chiefly, because that unto them were committed the oracles of God.
Romans 3:2

According to the glorious gospel of the blessed God, which was committed to my trust.
1 Timothy 1:11

God is Compassion

God being "full" of compassion is at maximum capacity. There is no greater amount possible. All compassion afforded man ultimately comes from God. This is an intimate love exclusive from God to Man. This is entirely fitting since the root word grace refers to the unmerited favor of God to man. This compassion is an expression of God's love.

The manifestation of God's healing is an act of compassion.

The example of God's treatment of Job was that of compassion. God was merciful in His dealings with Job. In God's compassion, He did not ascribe any liability to Job. It was God's compassion that caused Him to withhold judgment or punishment.

But thou, O Lord, art a God full of compassion, and gracious, long suffering, and plenteous in mercy and truth. Psalm 86:15

He hath made his wonderful works to be remembered: the Lord is gracious and full of compassion.

Psalm 111:4

The Lord is gracious, and full of compassion; slow to anger, and of great mercy.

Psalm 145:8

Howbeit Jesus suffered him not, but saith unto him, Go home to thy friends, and tell them how great things the Lord hath done for thee, and hath had compassion on thee.

Mark 5:19

Behold, we count them happy which endure. Ye have heard of the patience of Job, and have seen the end of the Lord; that the Lord is very pitiful, and of tender mercy.

James 5:11

I am Compassionate

Being compassionate sets aside any misconduct by the individual you are showing compassion for. The father of the prodigal son did not stop to first take inventory of all that had occurred since the son first left with his inheritance. A compassionate attitude is not based on meeting a set of requirements. Being compassionate is and unconditional expression of love.

Being compassionate toward others is in understanding we are all in the same boat. To be of one mind is the intangible connection we have with one another. When we stop to realize this and visualize circumstances from another person's perspective, this paves the way to compassion. Allowing for compassion, makes a difference in how we interact with each other.

———>●<———

And he arose, and came to his father. But when he was yet a great way off, his father saw him, and had compassion, and ran, and fell on his neck, and kissed him.
Luke 15:20

Finally, be ye all of one mind, having compassion one of another, love as brethren, be pitiful, be courteous:
1 Peter 3:8

And of some have compassion, making a difference:
Jude 1:22

God is Completeness

By definition, completeness lacks nothing. All that is required for 100% success is present. God never does anything in a halfhearted way. When God purposed to sanctify man, he did it completely. When God created man, He did so with perfection in mind. Nothing good was withheld, only God's best was afforded mankind. God is complete in all that He does. When God created the heavens and the earth, He declared that it was good; meaning nothing was absent that should have been there. Creation was perfect and complete in every aspect of the word.

The number seven symbolizes completeness in the individual: the perfection of the individual soul. The number twelve symbolizes corporate completeness.

———◄●►———

And the very God of peace sanctify you wholly; and I pray God your whole spirit and soul and body be preserved blameless unto the coming of our Lord Jesus Christ.
1 Thessalonians 5:23

And ye are complete in him, which is the head of all principality and power:
Colossians 2:10

Epaphras, who is one of you, a servant of Christ, saluteth you, always labouring fervently for you in prayers, that ye may stand perfect and complete in all the will of God.
Colossians 4:12

I am Complete

As a creation of God, I am also complete. Man is complete in Christ. As man alone could not satisfy his need for salvation, God completed that need in Christ. God's provision does not stop there. It is proper and fitting to say "I am completely cared for now and will always have my needs met according to Philippians 4:19."

We bear witness to our completeness in Christ, when we mirror the tenants of our faith that Jesus demonstrated to us.

Our life as a new creation is a work that began in us when we first came to Christ. The completeness is revealed as we exercise the truth of Gods word.

Studying the word of God puts us in closer connection with that completeness. There are no shortcuts. It is a lifetime of learning, and communing with the Lord.

Finally, brethren, farewell. Be perfect, be of good comfort, be of one mind, live in peace; and the God of love and peace shall be with you. 2 Corinthians 13:11

Epaphras, who is one of you, a servant of Christ, saluteth you, always labouring fervently for you in prayers, that ye may stand perfect and complete in all the will of God. Colossians 4:12

That the man of God may be perfect, thoroughly furnished unto all good works. 2 Timothy 3:17

But let patience have her perfect work, that ye may be perfect and entire, wanting nothing. James 1:4

God is Confidence

Confidence can only take form when all doubt is removed. God being confidence ensures this, since God is never about doubt or fear. The confidence we are to have concerning God is related to our salvation. If there is ever a doubt or fear directed to salvation, we are either calling God in to question (His integrity) or us relying on our own goodness to carry us through. It doesn't take much time of introspection to come to the conclusion that we fall short.

The Lord is said to be our confidence, because He is reliable. God is our confidence in every aspect of life. The confidence of God is even able to guard against us stumbling.

———⟶⊷⊶⟵———

By terrible things in righteousness wilt thou answer us, O God of our salvation; who art the confidence of all the ends of the earth, and of them that are afar off upon the sea:

Psalm 65:5

For the Lord shall be thy confidence, and shall keep thy foot from being taken.

Proverbs 3:26

I am Confident

I am confident in knowing that the message I speak is God's truth. There are no doubts, second-guessing or pause for concern. The confidence of the message is the confidence of God's truth.

I am confident in knowing that Jesus was who He claimed to be; the Son of God.

I am confident, it is Jesus' desire, that I bring any and all prayer requests before Him.

———————

I rejoice therefore that I have confidence in you in all things.
2 Corinthians 7:16

In whom we have boldness and access with confidence by the faith of him.
Ephesians 3:12

And we have confidence in the Lord touching you, that ye both do and will do the things which we command you.
2 Thessalonians 3:4

And now, little children, abide in him; that, when he shall appear, we may have confidence, and not be ashamed before him at his coming.
1 John 2:28

Beloved, if our heart condemn us not, then have we confidence toward God.
1John 3:21

And this is the confidence that we have in him, that, if we ask any thing according to his will, he heareth us:
1 John 5:14

God Delights in

God delights in doing good even when doing good is not warranted. God's mercy motivates Him toward the good He bestows on mankind. God delights in dealing justly with mankind. God delights in lives of those who are blameless. God delights in those who deal truthfully with others. God delights in hearing the prayers of the saints.

It is incumbent of us to be all of one mind; that the God of love and peace delights to dwell in us.

Who is a God like unto thee, that pardoneth iniquity, and passeth by the transgression of the remnant of his heritage? he retaineth not his anger for ever, because he delighteth in mercy.
Micah 7:18

A false balance is abomination to the Lord: but a just weight is his delight.
Proverbs 11:1

They that are of a froward heart are abomination to the Lord: but such as are upright in their way are his delight.
Proverbs 11:20

Lying lips are abomination to the Lord: but they that deal truly are his delight.
Proverbs 12:22

The sacrifice of the wicked is an abomination to the Lord: but the prayer of the upright is his delight.
Proverbs 15:8

I Delight in

I delight in the Almighty for His provision. I delight in God's law, that it always produces good and that I always benefit when meditating on it. I delight in knowing that my desires are God's concern. I revere God as I delight in His commandments.

———————

Yea, the Almighty shall be thy defence, and thou shalt have plenty of silver. For then shalt thou have thy delight in the Almighty, and shalt lift up thy face unto God.
Job 22:25-26

But his delight is in the law of the Lord; and in his law doth he meditate day and night.
Psalm 1:2

Delight thyself also in the Lord: and he shall give thee the desires of thine heart.
Psalm 37:4

I delight to do thy will, O my God: yea, thy law is within my heart.
Psalm 40:8

Praise ye the Lord. Blessed is the man that feareth the Lord, that delighteth greatly in his commandments.
Psalm 112:1

For I delight in the law of God after the inward man:
Romans 7:22

God is Discernment

Of the many qualities of God, among the highest valued is discernment. God represents discernment in its highest form. Compared to God's omnipotence, discernment is held in higher esteem. God was never hampered by the magnitude of power required to provide wealth for David. God's concern was "can you handle it?" When King Solomon asked for wisdom, he was asking God for discernment in handling all situations required of a just ruler. God knew the wisdom Solomon sought was the wisdom needed to manage great wealth. Solomon's wisdom allowed him to use the material blessings of God to benefit his kingdom. King Solomon did not squander the wealth. It is one thing to have wealth. It is infinitely better to first have discernment with wealth.

———◆———

And God said unto him, Because thou hast asked this thing, and hast not asked for thyself long life; neither hast asked riches for thyself, nor hast asked the life of thine enemies; but hast asked for thyself understanding to discern judgment; Behold, I have done according to thy words: lo, I have given thee a wise and an understanding heart; so that there was none like thee before thee, neither after thee shall any arise like unto thee.
1 Kings 3:11-12

For the word of God is quick, and powerful, and sharper than any twoedged sword, piercing even to the dividing asunder of soul and spirit, and of the joints and marrow, and is a discerner of the thoughts and intents of the heart.
Hebrews 4:12

I am Discerning

I am discerning between the righteous and the wicked. I am discerning between those who do and those who don't serve God.

I am discerning toward the Spirit of God.

I am only able to spiritually discern a matter based on my knowledge of Gods word. Through introspection, and mediation on God's word I am discerning of every condition that presents itself. I am discerning my own thoughts as measured against God's word.

Life lessons comprise a variety of scenes, which each season displays to the discerning eye.

Then shall ye return, and discern between the righteous and the wicked, between him that serveth God and him that serveth him not.
Malachi 3:18

But the natural man receiveth not the things of the Spirit of God: for they are foolishness unto him: neither can he know them, because they are spiritually discerned.
1 Corinthians 2:14

God is Empowerment

Gods omnipotence exalts Himself. Even God's voice carries with it the power and majesty of His Deity. God's infinite understanding is a demonstration of his power. Nothing in creation was beyond the power of God to realize. No limits can be placed on God's creative substance.

The message of the cross is a message of God's power.

The kingdom of God is not just a matter of idle talk or wishful thinking. The kingdom of God is the demonstration of God's power working in the lives of men.

———————

Behold, God exalteth by his power: who teacheth like him?
Job 36:22

The voice of the Lord is powerful; the voice of the Lord is full of majesty.
Psalm 29:4

Ah Lord God! behold, thou hast made the heaven and the earth by thy great power and stretched out arm, and there is nothing too hard for thee:
Jeremiah 32:17

For the preaching of the cross is to them that perish foolishness; but unto us which are saved it is the power of God.
1 Corinthians 1:18

For the kingdom of God is not in word, but in power.
1 Corinthians 4:20

To the only wise God our Saviour, be glory and majesty, dominion and power, both now and ever. Amen.
Jude 1:25

I am Empowered

I am empowered by the God of Israel.

I am empowered by the God who strengthened a nation.

I am empowered by the same God who gave kings strength and glory.

I am empowered to declare justice and might.

I am empowered to demonstrate signs and wonders by the Spirit of God.

I am empowered to preach the gospel of Christ.

The Holy Bible is my charter to square and circumscribe my actions, which empowers me for God's work.

God is my strength and power: and he maketh my way perfect.
2 Samuel 22:33

O God, thou art terrible out of thy holy places: the God of Israel is he that giveth strength and power unto his people. Blessed be God.
Psalm 68:35

Thou, O king, art a king of kings: for the God of heaven hath given thee a kingdom, power, and strength, and glory.
Daniel 2:37

But truly I am full of power by the spirit of the Lord, and of judgment, and of might, to declare unto Jacob his transgression, and to Israel his sin.
Micah 3:8

Through mighty signs and wonders, by the power of the Spirit of God; so that from Jerusalem, and round about unto Illyricum, I have fully preached the gospel of Christ.
Romans 15:19

God is Eternity

God has seen every generation of mankind. Every generation has seen the attributes of God. His eternal power and Godhead are undeniable. God is known as King eternal, immortal, invisible. God alone is wisdom, honor and glory forever.

God is eternity and through His grace has passed the gift of eternity to man. Just as God is eternity, He has made us partakers of his eternal glory through Christ Jesus.

———⇒●⇐———

The eternal God is thy refuge, and underneath are the everlasting arms: and he shall thrust out the enemy from before thee; and shall say, Destroy them.
Deuteronomy 33:27

Lord, thou hast been our dwelling place in all generations.
Psalm 90:1

Known unto God are all his works from the beginning of the world.
Acts 15:18

For the invisible things of him from the creation of the world are clearly seen, being understood by the things that are made, even his eternal power and Godhead; so that they are without excuse:
Romans 1:20

Now unto the King eternal, immortal, invisible, the only wise God, be honour and glory for ever and ever. Amen.
1 Timothy 1:17

But the God of all grace, who hath called us unto his eternal glory by Christ Jesus, after that ye have suffered a while, make you perfect, stablish, strengthen, settle you.
1 Peter 5:10

I am Eternal

I am eternal because of God. The knowledge of eternity and desire for eternity is place into the hearts of every man. When mans passes from this world, our eternity is even more sure than the reality we experience now. The belief in Christ assures us of this eternal state. There is no expiration date and no possibility that any force can affect this eternal state. God has secured our eternity and there is no greater force than God.

I shall see the King in the beauty of holiness, and with Him enter into an endless eternity.

He hath made every thing beautiful in his time: also he hath set the world in their heart, so that no man can find out the work that God maketh from the beginning to the end.

Ecclesiastes 3:11

And I give unto them eternal life; and they shall never perish, neither shall any man pluck them out of my hand.

John 10:28

For the wages of sin is death; but the gift of God is eternal life through Jesus Christ our Lord.

Romans 6:23

And this is the promise that he hath promised us, even eternal life.

1 John 2:25

And this is the record, that God hath given to us eternal life, and this life is in his Son.

1 John 5:11

Keep yourselves in the love of God, looking for the mercy of our Lord Jesus Christ unto eternal life.

Jude 1:21

God is Faithfulness

God is faithfulness and as such He covers all contingencies. God engulfs His creation with faithfulness. There is no escape from God's faithfulness. God is faithful in hearing our prayers and supplications. God is faithful to answer all of man's concerns. God's faithfulness includes the truth of His counsel.

God is faithful to even those who deny Him.

Thy mercy, O Lord, is in the heavens; and thy faithfulness reacheth unto the clouds.

Psalm 36:5

O Lord God of hosts, who is a strong Lord like unto thee? or to thy faithfulness round about thee?

Psalm 89:8

Hear my prayer, O Lord, give ear to my supplications: in thy faithfulness answer me, and in thy righteousness.

Psalm 143:1

O Lord, thou art my God; I will exalt thee, I will praise thy name; for thou hast done wonderful things; thy counsels of old are faithfulness and truth.

Isaiah 25:1

For what if some did not believe? shall their unbelief make the faith of God without effect?

Romans 3:3

I am Faithful

It is one thing to keep track of your own accomplishments and recount them to others. What God places a higher value on, is the man who is faithful in following His will. Taking care of a few things God has given to your charge, is evidence of being faithful. God does not entrust someone with a precious commodity until they have first proven faithful over something of lesser value.

God does not assign tasks of great importance to those who have proven to be unfaithful. God needs faithful men that can be trusted with properly impacting the lives of others.

I am faithful in communicating my faith to others.

God is looking to all men to have a faithful heart.

—————➤●◀—————

Most men will proclaim every one his own goodness: but a faithful man who can find?
Proverbs 20:6

His lord said unto him, Well done, thou good and faithful servant: thou hast been faithful over a few things, I will make thee ruler over many things: enter thou into the joy of thy lord.
Matthew 25:21

As we have therefore opportunity, let us do good unto all men, especially unto them who are of the household of faith.
Galatians 6:10

And the things that thou hast heard of me among many witnesses, the same commit thou to faithful men, who shall be able to teach others also.
2 Timothy 2:2

God is Freedom

God's love is a freeing love. Experiencing God's love is a freeing effect. The unconverted is likened to a prisoner. Once experiencing God's love there is a freedom in knowing God: one that allows man to live to the fullest. The restrictive feeling of prison no longer exists. It is replaced with the freeing knowledge of God's unconditional love.

God is absolute freedom.

Which executeth judgment for the oppressed: which giveth food to the hungry. The Lord looseth the prisoners:

Psalm 146:7

If the Son therefore shall make you free, ye shall be free indeed.

John 8:36

I am Free

Sin is the force that prevents us from being what God intended us to be. I can only be free when I am free from the law of sin and death. I am free when I deny this opposition to God's will. I am free when I renounce the lack of faith that wrought this plight of separation from God. I am set free from sin as my taskmaster. I am freed by Christ to be whatever I choose. I am free to be a slave of righteousness. This is true freedom.

I serve the Lord in freedom, fervency and zeal.

Being then made free from sin, ye became the servants of righteousness.

Romans 6:18

But now being made free from sin, and become servants to God, ye have your fruit unto holiness, and the end everlasting life.

Romans 6:22

For the law of the Spirit of life in Christ Jesus hath made me free from the law of sin and death.

Romans 8:2

God is Generosity

It is not enough for God to care for our salvation. God cares for our joy in the here and now. The joy of salvation is not just to be enjoyed after this life. It is God's desire that we experience the joy of salvation here on earth. There is no reason to worry or have angst toward anything. Our destiny is secured in the Lord. The Lord secures our provision for life on earth. What is there to fear? God's generosity is not rationed. There is not a percentage given now and the balance due at a later date. God's is generosity without limitations.

God in His generosity has given us principles to live by.

———⟫●⟪———

Restore unto me the joy of thy salvation; and uphold me with thy free spirit.

Psalm 51:12

For there is no difference between the Jew and the Greek: for the same Lord over all is rich unto all that call upon him.

Romans 10:12

For ye know the grace of our Lord Jesus Christ, that, though he was rich, yet for your sakes he became poor, that ye through his poverty might be rich.

2 Corinthians 8:9

I am Generous

I am generous and fear no lack because of it. Because I am generous, I will be made rich. He provides water to those who are in need. I receive water when I am in need. I watch for ways to be generous. I am generous to the poor. I am generous in creative ways. My generosity enables me to stand strong. I am generous in my prayers for others.

The liberal soul shall be made fat: and he that watereth shall be watered also himself.
Proverbs 11:25

He that hath a bountiful eye shall be blessed; for he giveth of his bread to the poor.
Proverbs 22:9

But the liberal deviseth liberal things; and by liberal things shall he stand.
Isaiah 32:8

A devout man, and one that feared God with all his house, which gave much alms to the people, and prayed to God alway.
Acts 10:2

God is Giver

God is a giver on many things. Among them are wisdom, understanding, largeness of heart, knowledge, skill in literature, understanding in visions and dreams, joy, kingdoms, majesty, glory, honor, and the increase in proselytizing.

———➤●◄———

And God gave Solomon wisdom and understanding exceeding much, and largeness of heart, even as the sand that is on the sea shore. 1 Kings 4:29

As for these four children, God gave them knowledge and skill in all learning and wisdom: and Daniel had understanding in all visions and dreams. Daniel 1:17

For God giveth to a man that is good in his sight wisdom, and knowledge, and joy: but to the sinner he giveth travail, to gather and to heap up, that he may give to him that is good before God. This also is vanity and vexation of spirit.
Ecclesiastes 2:26

O thou king, the most high God gave Nebuchadnezzar thy father a kingdom, and majesty, and glory, and honour:
Daniel 5:18

I have planted, Apollos watered; but God gave the increase.
1 Corinthians 3:6

And so it is written, The first man Adam was made a living soul; the last Adam was made a quickening spirit.
1 Corinthians 15:45

Every good gift and every perfect gift is from above, and cometh down from the Father of lights, with whom is no variableness, neither shadow of turning.
James 1:17

I am Giving

I am giving because this is what the Lord compels me to do. I must give to those in need when it is within my power to do so. Giving is baring the needs of self and family. I am giving as my ability will permit, without material injury to myself or family.

Giving is a process. It does not stop with one act. Giving is fluid and continual. Once you have initiated giving, it has a perpetual motion effect. Giving circulates good in this world. The giving principle is one of reciprocity: the one who gives will receive in like manner.

I am giving from my heart, not denying self. I am giving from the heart, not begrudging another. I am giving from the heart, not succumbing to a sales pitch. I am giving from my heart, which is cheerful in doing so.

———◆———

Withhold not good from them to whom it is due, when it is in the power of thine hand to do it.
Proverbs 3:27

Give, and it shall be given unto you; good measure, pressed down, and shaken together, and running over, shall men give into your bosom. For with the same measure that ye mete withal it shall be measured to you again.
Luke 6:38

Every man according as he purposeth in his heart, so let him give; not grudgingly, or of necessity: for God loveth a cheerful giver.
2 Corinthians 9:7

God is Glory

The glory of God is in the vastness of His creation. All that can be seen in the universe tells us there is no limit in number, no boundaries or limit creatively what God can manifest. There are no restrictions that can be imposed on God. Whatever the Mind of God thinks, it becomes so. There no such thing as limited supply with God. God has no limited resources. It is only mans limited thinking that cause limited results. God's glory is in limitless possibilities.

———————

The heavens declare the glory of God; and the firmament sheweth his handywork.
Psalm 19:1

Lift up your heads, O ye gates; and be ye lift up, ye everlasting doors; and the King of glory shall come in. Who is this King of glory? The Lord strong and mighty, the Lord mighty in battle. Lift up your heads, O ye gates; even lift them up, ye everlasting doors; and the King of glory shall come in. Who is this King of glory? The Lord of hosts, he is the King of glory. Selah.
Psalm 24:7-10

The voice of the Lord is upon the waters: the God of glory thundereth: the Lord is upon many waters.
Psalm 29:3

And he said, Men, brethren, and fathers, hearken; The God of glory appeared unto our father Abraham, when he was in Mesopotamia, before he dwelt in Charran,
Acts 7:2

I am Glorified

I am glorified because God ordained man's glory.

I am glorified because of the crucified Lord of glory.

All that I do is to be done with the glory of God in mind. There is no provision for anything less, second best, or failure.

I am glorified because man is the image and glory of God.

———————

But we speak the wisdom of God in a mystery, even the hidden wisdom, which God ordained before the world unto our glory: Which none of the princes of this world knew: for had they known it, they would not have crucified the Lord of glory.

1 Corinthians 2:7-8

Whether therefore ye eat, or drink, or whatsoever ye do, do all to the glory of God.

1 Corinthians 10:31

For a man indeed ought not to cover his head, forasmuch as he is the image and glory of God: but the woman is the glory of the man.

1 Corinthians 11:7

God is Goodness

God's goodness relegates to man always. God's goodness is available through every season of life. "All the days of my life" is both inclusive, of life on earth and in heaven. God's goodness is an eternal experience for mankind.

Surprisingly, it is God's goodness that draws men to Himself, not the prospect of damnation. It is God's goodness that convicts men of their need to repent.

The supreme and inscrutable artificer of the Universe has endeared Himself to the sons of men. We have discovered His power, wisdom, and goodness.

———————

Surely goodness and mercy shall follow me all the days of my life: and I will dwell in the house of the Lord for ever.

Psalm 23:6

Why boastest thou thyself in mischief, O mighty man? the goodness of God endureth continually.

Psalm 52:1

Or despisest thou the riches of his goodness and forbearance and longsuffering; not knowing that the goodness of God leadeth thee to repentance?

Romans 2:4

I am Good

God gives direction to men that can handle the task at hand: men that can follow orders. When God employs a man to do something it is ordered in steps. Only when you have successfully completed one step does the Lord give you the next step. We are good in not running ahead, but complying with the Lord at His pace.

Good men obtain favor from the Lord.

Good men plan for future generations.

Good men give what they treasure the most.

Good men and true, promote noble and glorious undertakings.

———————

The steps of a good man are ordered by the Lord: and he delighteth in his way.

Psalm 37:23

A good man obtaineth favour of the Lord: but a man of wicked devices will he condemn.

Proverbs 12:2

A good man leaveth an inheritance to his children's children: and the wealth of the sinner is laid up for the just.

Proverbs 13:22

A good man out of the good treasure of the heart bringeth forth good things: and an evil man out of the evil treasure bringeth forth evil things.

Matthew 12:35

For he was a good man, and full of the Holy Ghost and of faith: and much people was added unto the Lord.

Acts 11:24

For scarcely for a righteous man will one die: yet peradventure for a good man some would even dare to die. Romans 5:7

God is Grace

Grace is the unmerited favor we receive from God.

God's Grace was given Noah. God's grace was given to Jesus.

Do not underestimate God's Grace concerning the righteousness of man. God's grace was necessary for salvation. God's grace is available to all men.

⊸●⊷

But Noah found grace in the eyes of the Lord. Genesis 6:8

For the Lord God is a sun and shield: the Lord will give grace and glory: no good thing will he withhold from them that walk uprightly.

Psalm 84:11

And the child grew, and waxed strong in spirit, filled with wisdom: and the grace of God was upon him.

Luke 2:40

I do not frustrate the grace of God: for if righteousness come by the law, then Christ is dead in vain.

Galatians 2:21

For by grace are ye saved through faith; and that not of yourselves: it is the gift of God: Not of works, lest any man should boast.

Ephesians 2:8-9

For the grace of God that bringeth salvation hath appeared to all men,

Titus 2:11

Wherefore laying aside all malice, and all guile, and hypocrisies, and envies, and all evil speakings, As newborn babes, desire the sincere milk of the word, that ye may grow thereby: If so be ye have tasted that the Lord is gracious.

1 Peter 2:1-3

I am Gracious

I am gracious in caring for others. I use discretion in dividing my time between God & others; my vocation; and refreshment & sleep.

I am gracious when I speak.

I am gracious because of God working in my life.

I am gracious because of the manifold gifts of God.

A good man sheweth favour, and lendeth: he will guide his affairs with discretion.

Psalm 112:5

The words of a wise man's mouth are gracious; but the lips of a fool will swallow up himself.

Ecclesiastes 10:12

But by the grace of God I am what I am: and his grace which was bestowed upon me was not in vain; but I laboured more abundantly than they all: yet not I, but the grace of God which was with me.

1 Corinthians 15:10

As every man hath received the gift, even so minister the same one to another, as good stewards of the manifold grace of God.

1 Peter 4:10

God is Health

God is the source of all health.

God brings health and healing to mankind.

Healing is not an end to itself. Healing is a demonstration of God's peace and truth.

Although prosperity is commonly thought of in terms of finances, God's prosperity includes health.

God is interested in the prospering of our souls. This is true health, spiritual health.

For I will restore health unto thee, and I will heal thee of thy wounds, saith the Lord; because they called thee an Outcast, saying, This is Zion, whom no man seeketh after.

Jeremiah 30:17

Behold, I will bring it health and cure, and I will cure them, and will reveal unto them the abundance of peace and truth.

Jeremiah 33:6

Beloved, I wish above all things that thou mayest prosper and be in health, even as thy soul prospereth.

3 John 1:2

I am Healthy

Showing reverence to the Lord is one way of ensuring our health. God honors those with health and vigor who revere Him.

Those who speak wisdom promote their own health.

A faithful ambassador carries with him a message of good health.

A good report is a message of health.

Those who speak pleasant words apply health to the listener.

It is through health, vigor and the providence, that we should escape the numerous evils incident to childhood and youth, and realize a life indebted to God.

———⟫●⟪———

Be not wise in thine own eyes: fear the Lord, and depart from evil. It shall be health to thy navel, and marrow to thy bones.

Proverbs 3:7-8

There is that speaketh like the piercings of a sword: but the tongue of the wise is health.

Proverbs 12:18

A wicked messenger falleth into mischief: but a faithful ambassador is health.

Proverbs 13:17

The light of the eyes rejoiceth the heart: and a good report maketh the bones fat.

Proverbs 15:30

Pleasant words are as an honeycomb, sweet to the soul, and health to the bones.

Proverbs 16:24

God is Holiness

There is no other entity that compares to God's Holiness.
God is glorious in his presence.
God is to be revered.
God is to be praised.
God is performing wonders.
God proclaims His holiness.
It is the Spirit of holiness that is the power of the resurrection.

———⟫●⟨———

Who is like unto thee, O Lord, among the gods? who is like thee, glorious in holiness, fearful in praises, doing wonders?
Exodus 15:11

Give unto the Lord the glory due unto his name; worship the Lord in the beauty of holiness.
Psalm 29:2

God hath spoken in his holiness; I will rejoice, I will divide Shechem, and mete out the valley of Succoth.
Psalm 60:6

And declared to be the Son of God with power, according to the spirit of holiness, by the resurrection from the dead:
Romans 1:4

I am Holy

I am holy when I am cleansed of sin.

I am holy when I am made a new creation in Christ.

I am holy, as Christ has established my heart blameless before God the Father.

I am holy because God has called me to holiness.

I have been favored with new inducements, and I have been laid under new and stronger obligations of virtue and holiness.

May holiness to the Lord be engraved upon all our thoughts, words, and actions!

Having therefore these promises, dearly beloved, let us cleanse ourselves from all filthiness of the flesh and spirit, perfecting holiness in the fear of God.

2 Corinthians 7:1

And that ye put on the new man, which after God is created in righteousness and true holiness.

Ephesians 4:24

To the end he may stablish your hearts unblameable in holiness before God, even our Father, at the coming of our Lord Jesus Christ with all his saints.

1 Thessalonians 3:13

For God hath not called us unto uncleanness, but unto holiness.

1 Thessalonians 4:7

But as he which hath called you is holy, so be ye holy in all manner of conversation; Because it is written, Be ye holy; for I am holy.

1 Peter 1:15-16

God is Honor

Honor and majesty are the coverings of God. God's presence is that of honor and majesty.

Honor and glory are the hallmarks of God's work.

Honor from God is the only honor that matters. Self-honor means nothing.

God's honor is His Glory.

God's honor is the eternal, invisible wisdom of God.

———————

Bless the Lord, O my soul. O Lord my God, thou art very great; thou art clothed with honour and majesty.

Psalm 104:1

His work is honourable and glorious: and his righteousness endureth for ever.

Psalm 111:3

Jesus answered, If I honour myself, my honour is nothing: it is my Father that honoureth me; of whom ye say, that he is your God:

John 8:54

Now unto the King eternal, immortal, invisible, the only wise God, be honour and glory for ever and ever. Amen.

1 Timothy 1:17

I am Honorable

I am honorable when I do not procrastinate.

I am honorable as a man of my word.

I am honorable in victory.

I am honorable when I allow others to be treated with greater respect than myself.

All objects that man is charged to subserve are honorable and laudable.

———————

So the young man did not delay to do the thing, because he delighted in Jacob's daughter. He *was* more honorable than all the household of his father.

Genesis 34:19

And he said to him, "Look now, *there is* in this city a man of God, and *he is* an honorable man; all that he says surely comes to pass. So let us go there; perhaps he can show us the way that we should go."

1 Samuel 9:6

Now Naaman, commander of the army of the king of Syria, was a great and honorable man in the eyes of his master, because by him the Lord had given victory to Syria. He was also a mighty man of valor, *but* a leper.

2 Kings 5:1

When you are invited by anyone to a wedding feast, do not sit down in the best place, lest one more honorable than you be invited by him;

Luke 14:8

God is Hope

God is our hope and promise.
God's hope is joy and peace.
God's hope abounds by the power of the Holy Spirit.

Our hope in the Lord is more than just the thought of a small improvement in the quality of our lives. Hope personifies all the good that God is and the promise of that good toward mankind.

———————

For thou art my hope, O Lord God: thou art my trust from my youth.
Psalm 71:5

That they might set their hope in God, and not forget the works of God, but keep his commandments:
Psalm 78:7

Happy is he that hath the God of Jacob for his help, whose hope is in the Lord his God:
Psalm 146:5

And now I stand and am judged for the hope of the promise made of God, unto our fathers:
Acts 26:6

Now the God of hope fill you with all joy and peace in believing, that ye may abound in hope, through the power of the Holy Ghost.
Romans 15:13

I am Hopeful

My hope and trust is in the Lord.

I am hopeful there will be a resurrection of the just and unjust.

I am hopeful in the glory of God.

I am hopeful of eternal life.

I am hopeful toward the second coming of Christ.

May all our irregular passions be subdued, and may we daily increase in Faith, Hope, and Charity. May we enjoy the happy reflections consequent of a well-spent life, and the hope of eternal bliss.

For in thee, O Lord, do I hope: thou wilt hear, O Lord my God.
Psalm 38:15

Blessed is the man that trusteth in the Lord, and whose hope the Lord is.
Jeremiah 17:7

And have hope toward God, which they themselves also allow, that there shall be a resurrection of the dead, both of the just and unjust.
Acts 24:15

By whom also we have access by faith into this grace wherein we stand, and rejoice in hope of the glory of God.
Romans 5:2

In hope of eternal life, which God, that cannot lie, promised before the world began;
Titus 1:2

Looking for that blessed hope, and the glorious appearing of the great God and our Saviour Jesus Christ;
Titus 2:13

God is Joy

God is the oil or joy for mourning.
God is joy in Heaven when sinners repent.
God has provided us with healing, peace, abundance and joy. It is incumbent on us that we change our patterns of thought to accept our source of joy. Joy is a matter of being receptive to God's good in our lives.

---

for this day is holy unto our Lord: neither be ye sorry; for the joy of the Lord is your strength.
Nehemiah 8:10b

The Spirit of the Lord God is upon me; because the Lord hath anointed me to preach good tidings unto the meek; he hath sent me to bind up the brokenhearted, to proclaim liberty to the captives, and the opening of the prison to them that are bound; To proclaim the acceptable year of the Lord, and the day of vengeance of our God; to comfort all that mourn; To appoint unto them that mourn in Zion, to give unto them beauty for ashes, the oil of joy for mourning, the garment of praise for the spirit of heaviness; that they might be called trees of righteousness, the planting of the Lord, that he might be glorified. And they shall build the old wastes, they shall raise up the former desolations, and they shall repair the waste cities, the desolations of many generations.
Isaiah 61:1-4

I say unto you, that likewise joy shall be in heaven over one sinner that repenteth, more than over ninety and nine just persons, which need no repentance.
Luke 15:7

I am Joyful

I am joyful and rejoice in God's salvation.

I am joyful, being covered with God's robe of righteousness.

The will of God for us is to live in harmony, peace and joy. The fruit of these is realized through cultivating right thoughts.

God can only release His ideas into our consciousness when we are at peace with self and enjoying the experience of living.

Joyfulness is revealed in a new zest for doing what needs to be done: a life filled with enthusiasm.

And my soul shall be joyful in the Lord: it shall rejoice in his salvation.
Psalm 35:9

Make a joyful noise unto God, all ye lands:
Psalm 66:1

I will greatly rejoice in the Lord, my soul shall be joyful in my God; for he hath clothed me with the garments of salvation, he hath covered me with the robe of righteousness, as a bridegroom decketh himself with ornaments, and as a bride adorneth herself with her jewels.
Isaiah 61:10

Yet I will rejoice in the Lord, I will joy in the God of my salvation.
Habakkuk 3:18

God is Justice

God is justice accompanied with perfection, truth and righteousness.

God is without injustice.

God's justice cannot be perverted.

Seek God's justice.

Justice is that standard or boundary of right, which enables God to render to every man his just due. This virtue is not only consistent with Divine and human laws, but is the very cement and support of civil society. Justice, in a great measure, constitutes the reality of good in man.

———⟫●⟪———

He is the Rock, his work is perfect: for all his ways are judgment: a God of truth and without iniquity, just and right is he.

Deuteronomy 32:4

Yea, surely God will not do wickedly, neither will the Almighty pervert judgment.

Job 34:12

Learn to do well; seek judgment, relieve the oppressed, judge the fatherless, plead for the widow.

Isaiah 1:17

And therefore will the Lord wait, that he may be gracious unto you, and therefore will he be exalted, that he may have mercy upon you: for the Lord is a God of judgment: blessed are all they that wait for him.

Isaiah 30:18

I am Just

I am just, as I walk with God.

I am just, when I increase my learning.

I am just, when I show reverence to God.

I am just, because I have a good reputation.

I am just when I judge with candor, admonish with friendship, and reprehend judgment with justice.

⟶➤●◄⟵

These are the generations of Noah: Noah was a just man and perfect in his generations, and Noah walked with God.

Genesis 6:9

Give instruction to a wise man, and he will be yet wiser: teach a just man, and he will increase in learning.

Proverbs 9:9

And, behold, there was a man named Joseph, a counsellor; and he was a good man, and a just:

Luke 23:50

And they said, Cornelius the centurion, a just man, and one that feareth God, and of good report among all the nation of the Jews, was warned from God by an holy angel to send for thee into his house, and to hear words of thee.

Acts 10:22

God is Kindness

It is the king's pleasure to show the kindness of God.
God is abundant in kindness.
God is of great kindness.
Kindness is the handmaid of God's love and the reality of God in man.

———➤●◄———

And the king said, Is there not yet any of the house of Saul, that I may shew the kindness of God unto him? And Ziba said unto the king, Jonathan hath yet a son, which is lame on his feet.
2 Samuel 9:3

And refused to obey, neither were mindful of thy wonders that thou didst among them; but hardened their necks, and in their rebellion appointed a captain to return to their bondage: but thou art a God ready to pardon, gracious and merciful, slow to anger, and of great kindness, and forsookest them not.
Nehemiah 9:17

And rend your heart, and not your garments, and turn unto the Lord your God: for he is gracious and merciful, slow to anger, and of great kindness, and repenteth him of the evil.
Joel 2:13

But after that the kindness and love of God our Saviour toward man appeared, Not by works of righteousness which we have done, but according to his mercy he saved us, by the washing of regeneration, and renewing of the Holy Ghost; Which he shed on us abundantly through Jesus Christ our Saviour; That being justified by his grace, we should be made heirs according to the hope of eternal life.
Titus 3:4-7

I am Kind

God desires kindness in me.

I am kind to others, tenderhearted and forgiving.

As the elect of God, I am kind, merciful, humble, meek and longsuffering.

It is my province to recommend to my neighbor, kindness and condescension.

The desire of a man is his kindness: and a poor man is better than a liar.

Proverbs 19:22

And be ye kind one to another, tenderhearted, forgiving one another, even as God for Christ's sake hath forgiven you.

Ephesians 4:32

Put on therefore, as the elect of God, holy and beloved, bowels of mercies, kindness, humbleness of mind, meekness, longsuffering;

Colossians 3:12

God is Knowledge

All knowledge is measured against the knowledge of God. God's knowledge is not to be obscured to man, but will be understood as man fears God.

God's knowledge is a precious commodity: more so than any offering one can devise.

The depth of God's knowledge cannot be measured. It is as unquantifiable as His riches and wisdom.

God is all knowledge past and present.

Knowledge is not merely the accumulation of facts or skills, which inflates mans ego. The highest calling of knowledge transcends the intellect of man to afford spiritual redemption.

---

for the Lord is a God of knowledge, and by him actions are weighed.

1 Samuel 2:3b

Then shalt thou understand the fear of the Lord, and find the knowledge of God.

Proverbs 2:5

For I desired mercy, and not sacrifice; and the knowledge of God more than burnt offerings.

Hosea 6:6

O the depth of the riches both of the wisdom and knowledge of God! how unsearchable are his judgments, and his ways past finding out!

Romans 11:33

I am Knowing

Those who are wise, understanding and knowledgeable are best suited for leaders.

The lack of knowledge has devastating effects on a people. The rejection of knowledge acts like a destructive force that sweeps through a nation. This refers to knowledge paying homage to God, not secular teachings.

I am "knowing" when listening to the word of God as the way to gain true knowledge. I am "knowing" as draw closer to the knowledge of truth.

Take you wise men, and understanding, and known among your tribes, and I will make them rulers over you.

Deuteronomy 1:13

My people are destroyed for lack of knowledge: because thou hast rejected knowledge, I will also reject thee, that thou shalt be no priest to me: seeing thou hast forgotten the law of thy God, I will also forget thy children.

Hosea 4:6

As for these four children, God gave them knowledge and skill in all learning and wisdom: and Daniel had understanding in all visions and dreams.

Daniel 1:17

Awake to righteousness, and sin not; for some have not the knowledge of God: I speak this to your shame.

1 Corinthians 15:34

Who will have all men to be saved, and to come unto the knowledge of the truth.

1 Timothy 2:4

God is Life

God is both life and life-giving. All life proceeds from God.

Jesus, the bread of life, is the one who gives eternal life to the world. Those who come to Him will never hunger or thirst.

God is the eternal elixir of life who produces power and action at the impulse of thought.

———————

In whose hand is the soul of every living thing, and the breath of all mankind.

Job 12:10

All things were made by him; and without him was not any thing made that was made. In him was life; and the life was the light of men. And the light shineth in darkness; and the darkness comprehended it not.

John 1:3-5

Then Jesus said unto them, Verily, verily, I say unto you, Moses gave you not that bread from heaven; but my Father giveth you the true bread from heaven. For the bread of God is he which cometh down from heaven, and giveth life unto the world.

John 6:32-33

And Jesus said unto them, I am the bread of life: he that cometh to me shall never hunger; and he that believeth on me shall never thirst.

John 6:35

I am Living

The idea of life was first in the mind of God. God spoke all life into existence, and applied His own breath unique to the creation to man. God made man a living soul. God created man in His own image.

I am living a pure and blameless life, with a firm reliance on Divine Providence.

You can achieve whatever you want out of life, as long as you make God your partner in getting there.

———————

And the Lord God formed man of the dust of the ground, and breathed into his nostrils the breath of life; and man became a living soul.
Genesis 2:7

And so it is written, The first man Adam was made a living soul; the last Adam was made a quickening spirit.
1 Corinthians 15:45

God is Light

The first priority in God's creation was that of light. God being light; cannot impose His creation without the infusion of light. Light is God's signature on all things made.

Jesus declared that He is the light of the world. Light of the sun shines throughout the world. It does not discriminate like a laser beam. Jesus' light spreads to all of mankind. The Lord does not discriminate among men.

Darkness is the absence of God.

The Lamb of God (Jesus) is the light of the new Jerusalem.

In the beginning God created the heaven and the earth. And the earth was without form, and void; and darkness was upon the face of the deep. And the Spirit of God moved upon the face of the waters. And God said, Let there be light: and there was light.

Genesis 1:1-3

Then spake Jesus again unto them, saying, I am the light of the world: he that followeth me shall not walk in darkness, but shall have the light of life.

John 8:12

As long as I am in the world, I am the light of the world.

John 9:5

This then is the message which we have heard of him, and declare unto you, that God is light, and in him is no darkness at all.

1 John 1:5

And the city had no need of the sun, neither of the moon, to shine in it: for the glory of God did lighten it, and the Lamb is the light thereof. Revelation 21:23

I am Light

As the Spirit of God indwells man so does the Light of God. I am Light because God is light. I cannot separate myself from the love of God. Neither can I separate myself from the light of God. As a believer, I have been given the Holy Spirit in full measure. This light ministers to my spiritual health.

I am light as I demonstrate good works that glorify my heavenly Father.

I am light because "Christ in you, the hope of glory" is the light of all mankind.

Those who have been in darkness and seek to be brought to light, receive their part in the rights and benefits as a redeemed child of God.

I have even heard of thee, that the spirit of the gods is in thee, and that light and understanding and excellent wisdom is found in thee.
Daniel 5:14

Let your light so shine before men, that they may see your good works, and glorify your Father which is in heaven.
Matthew 5:16

In him was life; and the life was the light of men.
John 1:4

God is Mind

God is mind, and in the beginning was God. The mind of God is the progenitor of creation. When the mind of the Lord is shown to mankind, we have a glimpse of eternity. We are privy to all that God has ever thought. The mind of God is all accumulated knowledge. The natural world is a manifestation of God's mind.

Man's world includes the manifestation of Man's mind. What man has thought produced is a manifestation of mind. All that is designed and built is first borne in the mind of man.

The limitation of God's mind is one thing that can never be discovered.

It is God's mind that inspires us and arouses us toward a call to action.

——————<>●<>——————

And they put him in ward, that the mind of the Lord might be shewed them.

Leviticus 24:12

For who hath known the mind of the Lord? or who hath been his counsellor?

Romans 11:34

I am Mind

The mind of man is to be joined with infinite mind through Christ Jesus. The mind of Jesus is not just our creator; He is our salvation. Man is to be like-minded toward each other as we have the mind of Christ. Christ is our commonality. Christ is our oneness.

I am one with mind, which is the creative and eternal mind of God.

I can only act upon that which I entertain in my mind.

Idleness atrophies the mind; creative use expands all horizons.

———⇒●⇐———

Now the God of patience and consolation grant you to be likeminded one toward another according to Christ Jesus: That ye may with one mind and one mouth glorify God, even the Father of our Lord Jesus Christ. Romans 15:5-6

For who hath known the mind of the Lord, that he may instruct him? but we have the mind of Christ. 1 Corinthians 2:16

Finally, brethren, farewell. Be perfect, be of good comfort, be of one mind, live in peace; and the God of love and peace shall be with you. 2 Corinthians 13:11

Fulfil ye my joy, that ye be likeminded, having the same love, being of one accord, of one mind. Philippians 2:2

Let this mind be in you, which was also in Christ Jesus: Philippians 2:5

For God hath not given us the spirit of fear; but of power, and of love, and of a sound mind. 2 Timothy 1:7

Finally, be ye all of one mind, having compassion one of another, love as brethren, be pitiful, be courteous: 1 Peter 3:8

God is Order

God is order in it's purest from.

God's will is not a happenstance process. God's plan for man is ordered and has purpose.

Any time God admonishes man to ascribe to a standard, He is revealing that same attribute belongs to Him. God does require one behavior of man and something lessor of Himself. God always holds Himself to the highest standard. When Paul reminds the Corinthians that all things should be done "decently and in order" he is speaking concerning the will of God the Father.

———————

Although my house be not so with God; yet he hath made with me an everlasting covenant, ordered in all things, and sure: for this is all my salvation, and all my desire, although he make it not to grow.
2 Samuel 23:5

The steps of a good man are ordered by the Lord: and he delighteth in his way.
Psalm 37:23

Let all things be done decently and in order.
1 Corinthians 14:40

I am Ordered

The construction of King Solomon's Temple was performed as a well-ordered task. God gave specific instructions of material and form in building it. Nothing was left to private interpretation. There was no substituting of material to cut cost. There were no changes in dimensions to make it easier to build. The plans that Solomon used were well-ordered by God.

The work that man does for the Lord should be well-ordered.

All that man does should be done for the glory of God. That being the case, our worship, our conduct, our very presence in all that we do should represent our very best to God.

I am ordered in doing whatever I do, "heartily, as unto the Lord."

—————>•<—————

Now all the work of Solomon was prepared unto the day of the foundation of the house of the Lord, and until it was finished. So the house of the Lord was perfected.

2 Chronicles 8:16

And also the burnt offerings were in abundance, with the fat of the peace offerings, and the drink offerings for every burnt offering. So the service of the house of the Lord was set in order.

2 Chronicles 29:35

Whoso offereth praise glorifieth me: and to him that ordereth his conversation aright will I shew the salvation of God.

Psalm 50:23

And whatsoever ye do, do it heartily, as to the Lord, and not unto men; Knowing that of the Lord ye shall receive the reward of the inheritance: for ye serve the Lord Christ.

Colossians 3:23-24

God is Peace

The blessing from one believer to another should be that of peace. Shalom. In Christian parlance, the expression is simply "peace be with you."

God, not being the author of confusion is the author of peace. When we speak peace to another or offer peace to someone, we are in reality offering the peace of God. It is incumbent upon us to be mindful of the peace of God when communicating with others.

When we succumb to the peace of God it is then God sets us aside for a special purpose.

God's Peace is an outgrowth of God's wisdom.

———◆———

Now the God of peace be with you all. Amen.
Romans 15:33

For God is not the author of confusion, but of peace, as in all churches of the saints.
1 Corinthians 14:33

Those things, which ye have both learned, and received, and heard, and seen in me, do: and the God of peace shall be with you.
Philippians 4:9

And the very God of peace sanctify you wholly; and I pray God your whole spirit and soul and body be preserved blameless unto the coming of our Lord Jesus Christ.
1 Thessalonians 5:23

But the wisdom that is from above is first pure, then peaceable, gentle, and easy to be intreated, full of mercy and good fruits, without partiality, and without hypocrisy.
James 3:17

I am Peaceable

I am peaceable when I lead a quiet life that conforms to the laws of the land.

I am peaceable when I refrain from speaking evil of others.

I am peaceable when demonstrating gentleness, and humility in my dealings with others.

I am to be a quiet and peaceable citizen, true to my government, and just to my country. I am not to countenance disloyalty or rebellion, but patiently submit to legal authority.

I am to peaceably conform to the government of the country in which I live.

Take care that envy, discord, nor confusion are not allowed to interrupt universal peace and tranquility.

———❖———

For kings, and for all that are in authority; that we may lead a quiet and peaceable life in all godliness and honesty.

1 Timothy 2:2

To speak evil of no man, to be no brawlers, but gentle, shewing all meekness unto all men.

Titus 3:2

Now no chastening for the present seemeth to be joyous, but grievous: nevertheless afterward it yieldeth the peaceable fruit of righteousness unto them which are exercised thereby.

Hebrews 12:11

God is Perfection

God is perfection from the beginning of time. There is no sin in Him. God never misses the mark. God's way is perfect. It is the standard by which all other ways are compared.

God is perfection in justice.

God is perfection in truth.

God is perfection in righteousness.

God is perfection in word.

God is perfection in safety.

God is perfection in integrity.

God is perfection in beauty.

———⟶●⟵———

He is the Rock, his work is perfect: for all his ways are judgment: a God of truth and without iniquity, just and right is he.

Deuteronomy 32:4

As for God, his way is perfect; the word of the Lord is tried: he is a buckler to all them that trust in him.

2 Samuel 22:31

As for God, his way is perfect: the word of the Lord is tried: he is a buckler to all those that trust in him.

Psalm 18:30

Out of Zion, the perfection of beauty, God hath shined.

Psalm 50:2

I am Perfect

I am perfect as God's ambassador for this day and age.

God makes my way perfect.

I am perfect as I reflect the image of God.

I am perfectly bonded to almighty God through Jesus Christ.

I am perfected in God through His holy word.

The contemplative are lead to view with reverence and admiration, the glorious works of creation, which inspires them with the most exalted ideas of the perfections of their Divine Creator.

There is a state of perfection at which we hope to arrive by a virtuous education, our own endeavors, and the blessing of God.

These are the generations of Noah: Noah was a just man and perfect in his generations, and Noah walked with God.
Genesis 6:9

God is my strength and power: and he maketh my way perfect.
2 Samuel 22:33

It is God that girdeth me with strength, and maketh my way perfect. Psalm 18:32

Be ye therefore perfect, even as your Father which is in heaven is perfect. Matthew 5:48

And above all these things put on charity, which is the bond of perfectness.
Colossians 3:14

But whoso keepeth his word, in him verily is the love of God perfected: hereby know we that we are in him.
1 John 2:5

God is Pleasure

God takes pleasure in the prosperity of His servants.

God takes pleasure the spiritual health of his people.

God's pleasure is in the work He does in man's life.

God has given man the powers of reasoning, and capacity of improvement and pleasure.

Material thinking subverts spiritual vision and depletes mind of the creative process. It occupies the mind with thoughts of fear and robs us of God's good pleasure.

———————

Let them shout for joy, and be glad, that favour my righteous cause: yea, let them say continually, Let the Lord be magnified, which hath pleasure in the prosperity of his servant.

Psalm 35:27

For the Lord taketh pleasure in his people: he will beautify the meek with salvation.

Psalm 149:4

For it is God which worketh in you both to will and to do of his good pleasure.

Philippians 2:13

I am Pleasing

I am pleasing to God when I am fruitful in every good work.
I am pleasing to God as I increase in the knowledge of God.
I am pleasing to God as a child obedient to parents.
I am pleasing to God as a worker not disputing with his employer.
I am pleasing to God in every good work that I do.
I am pleasing to God as I keep His commandments.

Wherefore we labour, that, whether present or absent, we may be accepted of him.
2 Corinthians 5:9

That ye might walk worthy of the Lord unto all pleasing, being fruitful in every good work, and increasing in the knowledge of God;
Colossians 1:10

Children, obey your parents in all things: for this is well pleasing unto the Lord.
Colossians 3:20

Exhort servants to be obedient unto their own masters, and to please them well in all things; not answering again;
Titus 2:9

Make you perfect in every good work to do his will, working in you that which is wellpleasing in his sight, through Jesus Christ; to whom be glory for ever and ever. Amen.
Hebrews 13:21

And whatsoever we ask, we receive of him, because we keep his commandments, and do those things that are pleasing in his sight.
1 John 3:22

God is Plenty

God is plenty in all things from the subtlety of dew to the fatness of the earth. God is plenty in the sustenance He provides man. There is always enough to fill our every need and plenty in that God's supply never is depleted or runs low.

God is plenty for now and in the future. God adds to your good as the need increases.

God is plenty because there is enough for all, with a great abundance of supply remaining.

Just as the pomegranates, from the exuberance of their seed, denote plenty, so is the Lord's cornucopia.

———————

Therefore God give thee of the dew of heaven, and the fatness of the earth, and plenty of corn and wine:

Genesis 27:28

And the Lord shall make thee plenteous in goods, in the fruit of thy body, and in the fruit of thy cattle, and in the fruit of thy ground, in the land which the Lord sware unto thy fathers to give thee.

Deuteronomy 28:11

And Azariah the chief priest of the house of Zadok answered him, and said, Since the people began to bring the offerings into the house of the Lord, we have had enough to eat, and have left plenty: for the Lord hath blessed his people; and that which is left is this great store.

2 Chronicles 31:10

I am Plentiful

I am plentiful because God has blessed my diligent plans.

I am plentiful because I have placed work above frivolity.

I am plentiful in sustenance because the Lord has dealt wondrously with me.

The Lord has provided me a plentiful harvest to reap.

Plentiful is being rich in mind: knowing that whatever mind sees as a need, at any given moment, can and will be become that effect in the material world.

The thoughts of the diligent tend only to plenteousness; but of every one that is hasty only to want.

Proverbs 21:5

He that tilleth his land shall have plenty of bread: but he that followeth after vain persons shall have poverty enough.

Proverbs 28:19

And ye shall eat in plenty, and be satisfied, and praise the name of the Lord your God, that hath dealt wondrously with you: and my people shall never be ashamed.

Joel 2:26

Then saith he unto his disciples, The harvest truly is plenteous, but the labourers are few;

Matthew 9:37

God is Power

Whenever we are cognizant of God's power and speak of God's power He is exalted. Exalted in our reverence for Him and exalted in the Glories of Heaven.

God's power is immeasurable compared to the task at hand. There is nothing beyond the power of God.

God is power and demonstrates this infinite power through his infinite love of salvation for the Jew and the Greek.

God is power and by His very eternal nature, God's power cannot fade or be diminished.

Behold, God exalteth by his power: who teacheth like him?
Job 36:22

Ah Lord God! behold, thou hast made the heaven and the earth by thy great power and stretched out arm, and there is nothing too hard for thee:
Jeremiah 32:17

For I am not ashamed of the gospel of Christ: for it is the power of God unto salvation to every one that believeth; to the Jew first, and also to the Greek.
Romans 1:16

For the preaching of the cross is to them that perish foolishness; but unto us which are saved it is the power of God.
1 Corinthians 1:18

To the only wise God our Saviour, be glory and majesty, dominion and power, both now and ever. Amen.
Jude 1:25

I am Powerful

God is power and certainly the source of man's power. God gives each man the wherewithal to do as God intends. It is no accident that we have the skills and abilities that we enjoy. These are God given to fulfill God's purpose in our lives.

I am powerful because God makes my way perfect through His power.

I am powerful because God has gifted me with His power to do all that I am called to do.

———————

But thou shalt remember the Lord thy God: for it is he that giveth thee power to get wealth, that he may establish his covenant which he sware unto thy fathers, as it is this day.

Deuteronomy 8:18

God is my strength and power: and he maketh my way perfect. 2 Samuel 22:33

But when the multitudes saw it, they marvelled, and glorified God, which had given such power unto men.

Matthew 9:8

God is Prosperity

Prosperity is a work of God. It is not realized through mans efforts.

———————

And I came this day unto the well, and said, O Lord God of my master Abraham, if now thou do prosper my way which I go:
Genesis 24:42

And the Lord thy God will bring thee into the land which thy fathers possessed, and thou shalt possess it; and he will do thee good, and multiply thee above thy fathers.
Deuteronomy 30:5

This book of the law shall not depart out of thy mouth; but thou shalt meditate therein day and night, that thou mayest observe to do according to all that is written therein: for then thou shalt make thy way prosperous, and then thou shalt have good success.
Joshua 1:8

And keep the charge of the Lord thy God, to walk in his ways, to keep his statutes, and his commandments, and his judgments, and his testimonies, as it is written in the law of Moses, that thou mayest prosper in all that thou doest, and whithersoever thou turnest thyself:
1 Kings 2:3

And in every work that he began in the service of the house of God, and in the law, and in the commandments, to seek his God, he did it with all his heart, and prospered.
2 Chronicles 31:21

If they obey and serve him, they shall spend their days in prosperity, and their years in pleasures.
Job 36:11

I am Prosperous

I am prosperous when I seek the Lord, when I reverence the Lord, and when I pray for prosperity.

God takes pleasure in the prospering of His servants.

Man should engage his heart and tongue in promoting each other's welfare, and rejoicing in each other's prosperity.

———◦———

Now, my son, the Lord be with thee; and prosper thou, and build the house of the Lord thy God, as he hath said of thee.

1 Chronicles 22:11

And he sought God in the days of Zechariah, who had understanding in the visions of God: and as long as he sought the Lord, God made him to prosper.

2 Chronicles 26:5

What man is he that feareth the Lord? him shall he teach in the way that he shall choose. His soul shall dwell at ease; and his seed shall inherit the earth.

Psalm 25:12-13

Let them shout for joy, and be glad, that favour my righteous cause: yea, let them say continually, Let the Lord be magnified, which hath pleasure in the prosperity of his servant.

Psalm 35:27

Save now, I beseech thee, O Lord: O Lord, I beseech thee, send now prosperity.

Psalm 118:25

Beloved, I wish above all things that thou mayest prosper and be in health, even as thy soul prospereth.

3 John 1:2

God is Pureness

God is pureness. God's pureness is demonstrated in His words and in His commandments.

God is Pure in each of His attributes. God the Father is the Supreme Personality of the Universe, of which we ourselves are his offspring. We are raised in consciousness when we unify our own mentalities, in His pureness.

———————

The words of the Lord are pure words: as silver tried in a furnace of earth, purified seven times.

Psalm 12:6

With the merciful thou wilt shew thyself merciful; with an upright man thou wilt shew thyself upright; With the pure thou wilt shew thyself pure; and with the froward thou wilt shew thyself froward.

Psalm 18:25-26

The statutes of the Lord are right, rejoicing the heart: the commandment of the Lord is pure, enlightening the eyes.

Psalm 19:8

Every word of God is pure: he is a shield unto them that put their trust in him.

Proverbs 30:5

I am Pure

I am pure when I seek the Lord.

I am pure in conscience before the Lord.

I have a pure heart when calling on the Lord.

I am pure in faith when serving widows and orphans.

I am pure when seen as unspotted before the world.

Who shall ascend into the hill of the Lord? or who shall stand in his holy place? He that hath clean hands, and a pure heart; who hath not lifted up his soul unto vanity, nor sworn deceitfully. He shall receive the blessing from the Lord, and righteousness from the God of his salvation. This is the generation of them that seek him, that seek thy face, O Jacob. Selah.

Psalm 24:3-6

I thank God, whom I serve from my forefathers with pure conscience, that without ceasing I have remembrance of thee in my prayers night and day;

2 Timothy 1:3

Flee also youthful lusts: but follow righteousness, faith, charity, peace, with them that call on the Lord out of a pure heart.

2 Timothy 2:22

Pure religion and undefiled before God and the Father is this, To visit the fatherless and widows in their affliction, and to keep himself unspotted from the world.

James 1:27

God is Rejoicer

God is Rejoicer as we offer praise.
God is Rejoicer when we give thanks.
God is Rejoicer when we remember His holy name.

Rejoice in the Lord, O ye righteous: for praise is comely for the upright.
Psalm 33:1

Rejoice in the Lord, ye righteous; and give thanks at the remembrance of his holiness.
Psalm 97:12

I am Rejoiceful

I am rejoiceful toward the statutes of the Lord.

I am rejoiceful toward salvation.

I am rejoiceful being covered with the robe of righteousness.

I am rejoiceful in receiving the words of God.

I am rejoiceful in the coming of our Lord Jesus Christ.

The statutes of the Lord are right, rejoicing the heart: the commandment of the Lord is pure, enlightening the eyes.

Psalm 19:8

I will greatly rejoice in the Lord, my soul shall be joyful in my God; for he hath clothed me with the garments of salvation, he hath covered me with the robe of righteousness, as a bridegroom decketh himself with ornaments, and as a bride adorneth herself with her jewels.

Isaiah 61:10

Thy words were found, and I did eat them; and thy word was unto me the joy and rejoicing of mine heart: for I am called by thy name, O Lord God of hosts.

Jeremiah 15:16

Yet I will rejoice in the Lord, I will joy in the God of my salvation.

Habakkuk 3:18

Rejoice in the Lord always: and again I say, Rejoice.

Philippians 4:4

For what is our hope, or joy, or crown of rejoicing? Are not even ye in the presence of our Lord Jesus Christ at his coming? 1 Thessalonians 2:19

God is Riches

God is riches and it is only through God that man is given riches and wealth.

Man does not always know God's riches.

God's riches come unexpectedly.

God's riches given to man, draws men unto Himself.

God's riches are expressed in His goodness to man.

God's riches are given through His wisdom and knowledge.

Every man also to whom God hath given riches and wealth, and hath given him power to eat thereof, and to take his portion, and to rejoice in his labour; this is the gift of God.

Ecclesiastes 5:19

And I will give thee the treasures of darkness, and hidden riches of secret places, that thou mayest know that I, the Lord, which call thee by thy name, am the God of Israel.

Isaiah 45:3

Or despisest thou the riches of his goodness and forbearance and longsuffering; not knowing that the goodness of God leadeth thee to repentance?

Romans 2:4

O the depth of the riches both of the wisdom and knowledge of God! how unsearchable are his judgments, and his ways past finding out!

Romans 11:33

I am Rich

I am rich when humble before the Lord.

I am rich when I fear the Lord.

Jesus Christ's riches meets every need I have now, or will ever have in the future.

I am rich in assurance, understanding and knowledge through the Lord.

———>●<———

By humility and the fear of the Lord are riches, and honour, and life.
Proverbs 22:4

But my God shall supply all your need according to his riches in glory by Christ Jesus.
Philippians 4:19

To whom God would make known what is the riches of the glory of this mystery among the Gentiles; which is Christ in you, the hope of glory:
Colossians 1:27

That their hearts might be comforted, being knit together in love, and unto all riches of the full assurance of understanding, to the acknowledgement of the mystery of God, and of the Father, and of Christ;
Colossians 2:2

God is Righteousness

God is a righteousness that lasts forever. God's righteousness is revealed to man in faith, and through faith in Jesus Christ. God's righteousness is something we should know and understand. God's righteousness is in His law.

Revive me, O Lord, for Your name's sake! For Your righteousness' sake bring my soul out of trouble.
Psalm 143:11

Thus says the Lord: "Keep justice, and do righteousness, For My salvation *is* about to come, And My righteousness to be revealed.
Isaiah 56:1

O my people, remember now what Balak king of Moab consulted, and what Balaam the son of Beor answered him from Shittim unto Gilgal; that ye may know the righteousness of the Lord.
Micah 6:5

For therein is the righteousness of God revealed from faith to faith: as it is written, The just shall live by faith.
Romans 1:17

But now the righteousness of God without the law is manifested, being witnessed by the law and the prophets; Even the righteousness of God which is by faith of Jesus Christ unto all and upon all them that believe: for there is no difference:
Romans 3:21-22

For they being ignorant of God's righteousness, and going about to establish their own righteousness, have not submitted themselves unto the righteousness of God.
Romans 10:3

I am Righteous

I am righteous in the eyes of the Lord.
The Lord is my righteousness.
It is my righteousness that the Lord rewards.
I am judged by my righteousness and integrity.
I seek righteousness and humility.

—————————⟫●⟪—————————

The Lord rewarded me according to my righteousness: according to the cleanness of my hands hath he recompensed me.
2 Samuel 22:21

Therefore the Lord hath recompensed me according to my righteousness; according to my cleanness in his eye sight.
2 Samuel 22:25

Hear me when I call, O God of my righteousness: thou hast enlarged me when I was in distress; have mercy upon me, and hear my prayer.
Psalm 4:1

The Lord shall judge the people: judge me, O Lord, according to my righteousness, and according to mine integrity that is in me.
Psalm 7:8

The Lord rewarded me according to my righteousness; according to the cleanness of my hands hath he recompensed me.
Psalm 18:20

Seek ye the Lord, all ye meek of the earth, which have wrought his judgment; seek righteousness, seek meekness: it may be ye shall be hid in the day of the Lord's anger.
Zephaniah 2:3

For he hath made him to be sin for us, who knew no sin; that we might be made the righteousness of God in him. 2 Corinthians 5:21

God is Spirit

God is Spirit that first brought substance into form.

God is Spirit and being such gave power to create all things.

God is Spirit who responds only to spirit and truth. To worship God in spirit means: that we first must get a spiritual understanding of His nature. Spirit is that which cannot be destroyed or damaged. Matter can only be divided never individualized, as is the case with Divine Spirit. Your real self, the Christ within, the spiritual man, is an individualization of God. You are the presence of God at the point of your existence.

God is Spirit who leads His creation, the spirit of man.

———

And the earth was without form, and void; and darkness was upon the face of the deep. And the Spirit of God moved upon the face of the waters.

Genesis 1:2

Then he answered and spake unto me, saying, This is the word of the Lord unto Zerubbabel, saying, Not by might, nor by power, but by my spirit, saith the Lord of hosts.

Zechariah 4:6

God is a Spirit: and they that worship him must worship him in spirit and in truth.

John 4:24

For as many as are led by the Spirit of God, they are the sons of God.

Romans 8:14

I am Spirit

I am spirit, as I am made in the image of God. I am spirit and light just as God is Spirit and Light. God created me in Spirit and I will return to God as spirit. I am spirit as the Spirit of God dwells in me, which is the Spirit of Christ. I am spirit and have knowledge of God through my spirit. I am spirit, which is the temple of God. I am a part of that spiritual house of whom Christ is the Cornerstone.

=>●<=

The spirit of man is the candle of the Lord, searching all the inward parts of the belly.
Proverbs 20:27

Then shall the dust return to the earth as it was: and the spirit shall return unto God who gave it.
Ecclesiastes 12:7

But ye are not in the flesh, but in the Spirit, if so be that the Spirit of God dwell in you. Now if any man have not the Spirit of Christ, he is none of his.
Romans 8:9

For what man knoweth the things of a man, save the spirit of man which is in him? even so the things of God knoweth no man, but the Spirit of God.
1 Corinthians 2:11

Know ye not that ye are the temple of God, and that the Spirit of God dwelleth in you?
1 Corinthians 3:16

To whom coming, as unto a living stone, disallowed indeed of men, but chosen of God, and precious, Ye also, as lively stones, are built up a spiritual house, an holy priesthood, to offer up spiritual sacrifices, acceptable to God by Jesus Christ.
1 Peter 2:4-5

God is Strength

God's strength is the source of my strength.

God is the strength of my heart.

God is strength is always sufficient to accomplish whatever needs to be done.

God's strength is made perfect in weakness in that whatever man cannot do for himself, God's strength is more than sufficient to fill any need we might have. God's strength is the perfect compliment to man's weakness.

———⊸●⊷———

The Lord is my strength and song, and he is become my salvation: he is my God, and I will prepare him an habitation; my father's God, and I will exalt him.

Exodus 15:2

God is my strength and power: and he maketh my way perfect.

2 Samuel 22:33

Who is this King of glory? The Lord strong and mighty, the Lord mighty in battle.

Psalm 24:8

God is our refuge and strength, a very present help in trouble.

Psalm 46:1

O God, thou art terrible out of thy holy places: the God of Israel is he that giveth strength and power unto his people. Blessed be God.

Psalm 68:35

My flesh and my heart faileth: but God is the strength of my heart, and my portion for ever.

Psalm 73:26

I am Strong

I am strong because I trust in the Lord.
I am strong because God has armed me with strength.
I am strong as a rock.
I am strong through God's blessing.
I am strong in wisdom.
I am strong because the word of God abides in me.

———>●<———

The Lord is my rock, and my fortress, and my deliverer; my God, my strength, in whom I will trust; my buckler, and the horn of my salvation, and my high tower.
Psalm 18:2

It is God that girdeth me with strength, and maketh my way perfect.
Psalm 18:32

In God is my salvation and my glory: the rock of my strength, and my refuge, is in God.
Psalm 62:7

Blessed is the man whose strength is in thee; in whose heart are the ways of them.
Psalm 84:5

A wise man is strong; yea, a man of knowledge increaseth strength.
Proverbs 24:5

I have written unto you, fathers, because ye have known him that is from the beginning. I have written unto you, young men, because ye are strong, and the word of God abideth in you, and ye have overcome the wicked one.
1 John 2:14

God is Substance

God is substance, not to be confused with religious practices. Man judges one another with respect to compliance with dietary laws, habits, rituals and feasts. These are not substitutes for substance. Christ is more than an idea to be glibly spoken of, or over-spiritualized. Christ in His deity is substance. Christ is the reality of substance.

Faith is a construct of belief. Faith is not an entity in and of itself. Faith alone knows nothing and is impartial. Faith in Christ is entirely different. Jesus Christ, being the creative mind that formed all things, is the life force of man. Faith, which is first formed in mind, is unseen. It's evidence is realized in substance taking form. God manifests Himself through substance and so man's ideas are manifest through substance. Faith is the idea of what our reality will become.

Substance should not be confused with matter. Spirit is substance which can never wear or decay.

———⟫●⟪———

Bless, Lord, his substance, and accept the work of his hands; smite through the loins of them that rise against him, and of them that hate him, that they rise not again.
Deuteronomy 33:11

Let no man therefore judge you in meat, or in drink, or in respect of an holyday, or of the new moon, or of the sabbath days: Which are a shadow of things to come; but the body is of Christ.
Colossians 2:16-17

Now faith is the substance of things hoped for, the evidence of things not seen.
Hebrews 11:1

I am Substance

I am substance that was first an idea in the mind of God. God's creative thought gave way to substance forming the reality of man.

What makes man an eternal being in God's creation is that mankind is Spirit Substance. There is never a time when Spirit will not exist: both Divine Spirit and Man's spirit are substance.

I am Divine Substance composed in a spiritual world which demonstrates the reality of God.

Thine eyes did see my substance, yet being unperfect; and in thy book all my members were written, which in continuance were fashioned, when as yet there was none of them.

Psalm 139:16

Honour the Lord with thy substance, and with the firstfruits of all thine increase: So shall thy barns be filled with plenty, and thy presses shall burst out with new wine.

Proverbs 3:9-10

And Joanna the wife of Chuza Herod's steward, and Susanna, and many others, which ministered unto him of their substance.

Luke 8:3

For ye had compassion of me in my bonds, and took joyfully the spoiling of your goods, knowing in yourselves that ye have in heaven a better and an enduring substance.

Hebrews 10:34

God is Truth

God is truth and only truth. God cannot be anything less than truth. There can be no truer truth than God's truth.

Redemption is an outworking of truth. The lack of truth requires redemption.

To receive the word of God is to receive the word of Truth. They are one in the same and can not be separated.

God is truth, and man's quest for knowledge is what draws him to the truth of God.

He is the Rock, his work is perfect: for all his ways are judgment: a God of truth and without iniquity, just and right is he.

Deuteronomy 32:4

Into thine hand I commit my spirit: thou hast redeemed me, O Lord God of truth.

Psalm 31:5

That he who blesseth himself in the earth shall bless himself in the God of truth; and he that sweareth in the earth shall swear by the God of truth; because the former troubles are forgotten, and because they are hid from mine eyes.

Isaiah 65:16

For this cause also thank we God without ceasing, because, when ye received the word of God which ye heard of us, ye received it not as the word of men, but as it is in truth, the word of God, which effectually worketh also in you that believe.

1 Thessalonians 2:13

Who will have all men to be saved, and to come unto the knowledge of the truth. 1 Timothy 2:4

I am Truthful

I am truthful because I fear God.
I am truthful in executing judgment.
The truth of God has purified my soul.
Truth is a divine attribute, and the foundation of every virtue. To be good and true are among the first lessons we learn.

Moreover thou shalt provide out of all the people able men, such as fear God, men of truth, hating covetousness; and place such over them, to be rulers of thousands, and rulers of hundreds, rulers of fifties, and rulers of tens:
Exodus 18:21

Run ye to and fro through the streets of Jerusalem, and see now, and know, and seek in the broad places thereof, if ye can find a man, if there be any that executeth judgment, that seeketh the truth; and I will pardon it.
Jeremiah 5:1

These are the things that ye shall do; Speak ye every man the truth to his neighbour; execute the judgment of truth and peace in your gates:
Zechariah 8:16

Seeing ye have purified your souls in obeying the truth through the Spirit unto unfeigned love of the brethren, see that ye love one another with a pure heart fervently: Being born again, not of corruptible seed, but of incorruptible, by the word of God, which liveth and abideth for ever.
1 Peter 1:22-23

God is Understanding

God's understanding is mighty.

God is understanding is in knowing mans activities and thoughts.

God's understanding is unsearchable.

God's understanding in known through intimate communion with Him, which yields both power and results.

Right understanding of God is the basis for mans inner security.

Understanding God removes all guilt from the consciousness of man and permits streamlined thinking.

Behold, God is mighty, and despiseth not any: he is mighty in strength and wisdom.

Job 36:5

Thou knowest my downsitting and mine uprising, thou understandest my thought afar off.

Psalm 139:2

Great is our Lord, and of great power: his understanding is infinite.

Psalm 147:5

For the Lord giveth wisdom: out of his mouth cometh knowledge and understanding.

Proverbs 2:6

The Lord by wisdom hath founded the earth; by understanding hath he established the heavens.

Proverbs 3:19

Hast thou not known? hast thou not heard, that the everlasting God, the Lord, the Creator of the ends of the earth, fainteth not, neither is weary? there is no searching of his understanding.

Isaiah 40:28

I am Understanding

Understanding is the practical component of wisdom. I am understanding in keeping the law of God. I am understanding in praising God. I am understanding of visions and dreams.

—————➤●◄—————

And God gave Solomon wisdom and understanding exceeding much, and largeness of heart, even as the sand that is on the sea shore.
　1 Kings 4:29

Only the Lord give thee wisdom and understanding, and give thee charge concerning Israel, that thou mayest keep the law of the Lord thy God.
　1 Chronicles 22:12

For God is the King of all the earth: sing ye praises with understanding.
　Psalm 47:7

I have even heard of thee, that the spirit of the gods is in thee, and that light and understanding and excellent wisdom is found in thee.
　Daniel 5:14

That their hearts might be comforted, being knit together in love, and unto all riches of the full assurance of understanding, to the acknowledgement of the mystery of God, and of the Father, and of Christ;
　Colossians 2:2

And we know that the Son of God is come, and hath given us an understanding, that we may know him that is true, and we are in him that is true, even in his Son Jesus Christ. This is the true God, and eternal life.
　1 John 5:20

God is Wealth

God is wealth and holds the power for man to obtain wealth.

God is riches and wealth, and the giver of these to man.

God is omnipresent Wealth: the Infinite Riches of the Universe, ever expanding and increasing.

Christ is the incarnation of the wealth of the universe.

God's wealth is afforded man for the purpose of grand living. God is not parsimonious or stingy when it comes to providing for His creation. God is only capable of providing the best. With God there is no second best, therefore there can be no such thing as limited wealth.

But thou shalt remember the Lord thy God: for it is he that giveth thee power to get wealth, that he may establish his covenant which he sware unto thy fathers, as it is this day.

Deuteronomy 8:18

Every man also to whom God hath given riches and wealth, and hath given him power to eat thereof, and to take his portion, and to rejoice in his labour; this is the gift of God.

Ecclesiastes 5:19

I am Wealthy

I am wealthy in riches and righteousness forever, by the will of God. I have wealth and riches according to the will of God. I am wealthy when I have gathered my gain through labor.

Wealth is not a substitute for security of the Lord.

Wealth is the acquisition of goods and services produced by mankind, all of which originated in the mind of man. Wealth represents the intellect, ingenuity and industry of man fashioned from the world's natural resources.

Obtaining wealth is a means of realizing life's fullest potential. Wealth enables man to expand his influence for good in life. Creating wealth elevates the dignity of life.

I am made in the image of omnipresent wealth.

I am grateful, and thankful for all the wealth and abundance I am experiencing.

---

seeking the wealth of his people, and speaking peace to all his seed.
Ester 10:3b

Wealth and riches shall be in his house: and his righteousness endureth for ever.
Psalm 112:3

That I may cause those that love me to inherit substance; and I will fill their treasures.
Proverbs 8:21

Wealth gotten by vanity shall be diminished: but he that gathereth by labour shall increase.
Proverbs 13:11

God is Wisdom

God is infinite wisdom, the Intelligence that operates through everything, visible and invisible.

The indwelling Spirit of God teaches me the ways of wisdom and directs me to all good. It is the inner witness of His love and truth.

When our affairs are managed by Love, and directed by Wisdom; they are sure to prosper.

With him is wisdom and strength, he hath counsel and understanding. Job 12:13

O Lord, how manifold are thy works! in wisdom hast thou made them all: the earth is full of thy riches.
Proverbs 104:24

For wisdom is a defence, and money is a defence: but the excellency of knowledge is, that wisdom giveth life to them that have it. Ecclesiastes 7:12

Then said I, Wisdom is better than strength: Ecclesiastes 9:16a

but wisdom is profitable to direct. Ecclesiastes 10:10b

Thus saith the Lord God; Thou sealest up the sum, full of wisdom, and perfect in beauty. Ezekiel 28:12b

But unto them which are called, both Jews and Greeks, Christ the power of God, and the wisdom of God. 1 Corinthians 1:24

Saying with a loud voice, Worthy is the Lamb that was slain to receive power, and riches, and wisdom, and strength, and honour, and glory, and blessing. Revelation 5:12

I am Wise

With the stages of life: youth, manhood, and age, are their corresponding principles: beauty, strength and wisdom. The noblest of these is wisdom. "Wisdom is the principal thing; therefore get wisdom: and with all thy getting get understanding." Proverbs 4:7

———————

Only by pride cometh contention: but with the well advised is wisdom.
Proverbs 13:10

For God giveth to a man that is good in his sight wisdom, and knowledge, and joy: but to the sinner he giveth travail, to gather and to heap up, that he may give to him that is good before God. This also is vanity and vexation of spirit.
Ecclesiastes 2:26a

And the child grew, and waxed strong in spirit, filled with wisdom: and the grace of God was upon him.
Luke 2:40

Wherefore, brethren, look ye out among you seven men of honest report, full of the Holy Ghost and wisdom, whom we may appoint over this business. But we will give ourselves continually to prayer, and to the ministry of the word.
Acts 6:3-4

Let the word of Christ dwell in you richly in all wisdom; teaching and admonishing one another in psalms and hymns and spiritual songs, singing with grace in your hearts to the Lord.
Colossians 3:16

If any of you lack wisdom, let him ask of God, that giveth to all men liberally, and upbraideth not; and it shall be given him.
James 1:5

God is Witness

God is a true witness.

Jesus bore witness of Himself that the words He spoke and the claims He made concerning Himself were true.

God is witness through the Holy Spirit.

God is faithful and has been a true witness since the beginning of creation.

———⟶⟵———

There is another that beareth witness of me; and I know that the witness which he witnesseth of me is true.

John 5:32

Jesus answered and said unto them, Though I bear record of myself, yet my record is true: for I know whence I came, and whither I go; but ye cannot tell whence I come, and whither I go.

John 8:14

Whereof the Holy Ghost also is a witness to us: for after that he had said before,

Hebrews 10:15

And unto the angel of the church of the Laodiceans write; These things saith the Amen, the faithful and true witness, the beginning of the creation of God;

Revelation 3:14

I am Witnessing

I am witnessing indiscriminately to both the small and great. I am witnessing as I have received power from the Holy Spirit. As a believer, I am a witness to the resurrection of Jesus Christ. I am witnessing among the brethren and corroborating the truth of God.

———————

But ye shall receive power, after that the Holy Ghost is come upon you: and ye shall be witnesses unto me both in Jerusalem, and in all Judaea, and in Samaria, and unto the uttermost part of the earth.
Acts 1:8

This Jesus hath God raised up, whereof we all are witnesses.
Acts 2:32

Having therefore obtained help of God, I continue unto this day, witnessing both to small and great, saying none other things than those which the prophets and Moses did say should come:
Acts 26:22

This is the third time I am coming to you. In the mouth of two or three witnesses shall every word be established.
2 Corinthians 13:1

And the things that thou hast heard of me among many witnesses, the same commit thou to faithful men, who shall be able to teach others also.
2 Timothy 2:2

Wherefore seeing we also are compassed about with so great a cloud of witnesses, let us lay aside every weight, and the sin which doth so easily beset us, and let us run with patience the race that is set before us,
Hebrews 12:1

God is Wholeness

Wholeness is the absence of any and all maladies.

The whole counsel of God is capsulized in the life of Christ.

There are six elements of protection that comprise the whole armor of God which are: truth, righteousness, the gospel of peace, faith, salvation, and the word of God.

———————

Insomuch that the multitude wondered, when they saw the dumb to speak, the maimed to be whole, the lame to walk, and the blind to see: and they glorified the God of Israel.

    Matthew 15:31

For I have not shunned to declare unto you all the counsel of God.

    Acts 20:27

Put on the whole armour of God, that ye may be able to stand against the wiles of the devil. For we wrestle not against flesh and blood, but against principalities, against powers, against the rulers of the darkness of this world, against spiritual wickedness in high places. Wherefore take unto you the whole armour of God, that ye may be able to withstand in the evil day, and having done all, to stand.

    Ephesians 6:11-13

I am Whole

Peter testified before the rulers and elders of Israel that he was whole due to the work of Jesus Christ.

I am whole in my being of spirit, soul and body. All of which, created of God, are maintained by God. I am whole, because the Lord Jesus Christ declares me blameless.

———◦———

Be it known unto you all, and to all the people of Israel, that by the name of Jesus Christ of Nazareth, whom ye crucified, whom God raised from the dead, even by him doth this man stand here before you whole.

Acts 4:10

And the very God of peace sanctify you wholly; and I pray God your whole spirit and soul and body be preserved blameless unto the coming of our Lord Jesus Christ.

1 Thessalonians 5:23

CHAPTER 4

The Trifecta of God's and Man's Attributes

It is recorded in Revelation 4:1 that God created all things (including man) for His pleasure. Even so, man is not merely entertainment for God. We are created that God might live vicariously through us. That is God's pleasure. In doing so, God needs us to make ourselves available. God did not created us as a pre-programed robot with indifference. Man has dreams, desires, likes and dislikes, just as our creator God. We are indeed created for God's pleasure, but more importantly that we might be recipients of His great love. Without man, God has no way to communicate His love. Without man, God's very nature is unknown to the universe.

Man is not created to merely observe and record the workings of God in the lives of men. Man is to learn and live what it means to be created in the image of God. Man is to demonstrate that he is all that God has intended him to be.

All matter is subject to the will and desire of God. Man was once an idea in the mind of God. What God thinks must exist. God's idea was manifest in creation. What God plans must come to fruition. When God speaks, His word will not return void. It must be acted on.

When God created man in His image, man took on the form of God's creative nature. All that man has been accomplished on earth, was first an idea. Man used reason and experimentation to devise and develop all of the technological we enjoy today. Our ability to learn, remember and record valuable information has allowed us to make tremendous strides generation after generation. Man is continually growing in knowledge and abilities.

We share in God's attributes that we might act on them and realize a life of abundance, a life that that exemplifies our creative image of God.

God is Blessing

The first blessing God gave to man was the blessing of reproduction. Having offspring is a blessing that your life, your legacy will be carried on through successive generations.

God set aside the seventh day for a special purpose. God set the example. God sanctified the seventh day of the week to be a blessing to mankind. It is to be a time of Rest and refreshment from a week's worth of labor. It is also a time especially reserved for the meditation and worship. We are to ponder the majesty and goodness of Gods creation.

———⟫●⟪———

And God blessed them, saying, Be fruitful, and multiply, and fill the waters in the seas, and let fowl multiply in the earth.
Genesis 1:22

And God blessed them, and God said unto them, Be fruitful, and multiply, and replenish the earth, and subdue it: and have dominion over the fish of the sea, and over the fowl of the air, and over every living thing that moveth upon the earth.
Genesis 1:28

And God blessed the seventh day, and sanctified it: because that in it he had rested from all his work which God created and made.
Genesis 2:3

And God blessed Noah and his sons, and said unto them, Be fruitful, and multiply, and replenish the earth.
Genesis 9:1

He that hath clean hands, and a pure heart; who hath not lifted up his soul unto vanity, nor sworn deceitfully. He shall receive the blessing from the Lord, and righteousness from the God of his salvation.
Psalm 24:4-6

I am Blessed

There is blessing in both avoiding bad influences and embracing the teachings of God. We are told not to follow the advice or ways of the ungodly, but rather the advice and ways of the Lord. God's law teaches us wrong from right; that which brings detriment from that which enables us to prosper; and behavior that yields shameful consequences or promotes integrity.

———◆———

Blessed is the man that walketh not in the counsel of the ungodly, nor standeth in the way of sinners, nor sitteth in the seat of the scornful. But his delight is in the law of the Lord; and in his law doth he meditate day and night.
Psalm 1:1-2

O taste and see that the Lord is good: blessed is the man that trusteth in him.
Psalm 34:8

Blessed is the man whom thou chastenest, O Lord, and teachest him out of thy law;
Psalm 94:12

Praise ye the Lord. Blessed is the man that feareth the Lord, that delighteth greatly in his commandments.
Psalm 112:1

Blessed is the man that trusteth in the Lord, and whose hope the Lord is.
Jeremiah 17:7

Blessed is the man to whom the Lord will not impute sin.
Romans 4:8
Blessed is the man that endureth temptation: for when he is tried, he shall receive the crown of life, which the Lord hath promised to them that love him. James 1:12

I Bless

Once you spend time meditating on God's law you will begin to understand the benefits. You will intrinsically know that ALL is designed to produce Good in your life. God never gives instructions or requires man to do anything that produces pain or discomfort.

As meditation on God's law brings delight to the soul of man it also becomes the grounds for edification. In our quest to learn more of God and know his statutes we are now in a better position to influence others. We bless others with the joy and confidence we have received from the Lord. When we are blessed of the Lord, others are drawn to that good and conclude, "I want what he has."

No one is attracted to mediocrity or substandard anything. Be the best you can be for the glory of God. When you wear the label of a religion, make sure you are representing it in the most positive light; something others would find attractive and aspire to be a part of.

We are to bless others with positive affirmations about God and His desire for good in the lives of all people. "so is a man to his praise" Proverbs 27:21

———————

And the Lord spake unto Moses, saying, Speak unto Aaron and unto his sons, saying, On this wise ye shall bless the children of Israel, saying unto them, The Lord bless thee, and keep thee:

The Lord make his face shine upon thee, and be gracious unto thee: The Lord lift up his countenance upon thee, and give thee peace. And they shall put my name upon the children of Israel, and I will bless them.

Numbers 6:22-27

God is Comforter

If God is not able to comfort who is? It is the God of all comfort who best understands man, his failings, his capabilities and expresses his need for comfort. God in His mercy is the God of all comfort. This was demonstrated in the life of Jesus. There was never a person who demonstrated compassion and comfort, as did Jesus.

The Lord has compassion on the children of His creation; administering them comfort in time of trouble.

Yea, though I walk through the valley of the shadow of death, I will fear no evil: for thou art with me; thy rod and thy staff they comfort me.

Psalm 23:4

Blessed be God, even the Father of our Lord Jesus Christ, the Father of mercies, and the God of all comfort;

2 Corinthians 1:3

Now the God of patience and consolation grant you to be likeminded one toward another according to Christ Jesus: That ye may with one mind and one mouth glorify God, even the Father of our Lord Jesus Christ.

Romans 15:5-6

I am Comforted

It is the good that God demonstrates in our lives that brings comfort to our soul.

Knowledge of God's gift of redemption is cause for comfort. It is also cause to rejoice in song and praise to the Lord.

There is a seeming irony with regard to God's comfort. We are told that the fear of the Lord is related to comfort. This "fear" is the reverence man has for God. This is not fear as in the expectancy of impending danger. Revering God and knowing that He has our best interest at hand is a wonderfully comforting thought. It is God's Holy Spirit that gives us the assurance that all is well, all is under control, and we should <u>not</u> fear anything.

Our hearts should continually glow with gratitude to the great and beneficent Author of our existence, for the manifold blessings and comforts we enjoy.

——————

Shew me a token for good; that they which hate me may see it, and be ashamed: because thou, Lord, hast holpen me, and comforted me.
Psalm 86:17

Break forth into joy, sing together, ye waste places of Jerusalem: for the Lord hath comforted his people, he hath redeemed Jerusalem.
Isaiah 52:9

Then had the churches rest throughout all Judaea and Galilee and Samaria, and were edified; and walking in the fear of the Lord, and in the comfort of the Holy Ghost, were multiplied.
Acts 9:31

I am Comforting

It is only through the power of God that we have the ability to comfort others. God comes to us in times of tribulation and comforts us with His Spirit. This same comfort is seen in our sprit and affects those we encounter who are in distress. Our calmness: our assurance that all is being cared for, is the comfort that others see and receive.

It is our duty as friends to minister to those distresses, and comfort their afflictions.

Blessed be God, even the Father of our Lord Jesus Christ, the Father of mercies, and the God of all comfort; Who comforteth us in all our tribulation, that we may be able to comfort them which are in any trouble, by the comfort wherewith we ourselves are comforted of God.

2 Corinthians 1:3-4

Nevertheless God, that comforteth those that are cast down, comforted us by the coming of Titus; And not by his coming only, but by the consolation wherewith he was comforted in you, when he told us your earnest desire, your mourning, your fervent mind toward me; so that I rejoiced the more.

2 Corinthians 7:6-7

God is Demonstrator

The demonstration of Jesus was in His righteousness. This demonstration confirmed that He was God in the flesh, He alone was sent for the purpose of reconciling mankind to God, and His demonstration is definitive. His blood sacrifice was sufficient for the redemption for all of mankind, now and through the ages. There will never come a time when another sacrifice is needed. There is no expiration date on the work of Christ. God has demonstrated that He, and He alone is all sufficient for the needs of mankind.

Christ became the demonstration to man because of man's sin, not because of man's goodness. The greatest demonstration of love was in Christ giving of Himself all that He had (life on earth) to a people who were by practice and by nature, unloving.

Even the righteousness of God which is by faith of Jesus Christ unto all and upon all them that believe: for there is no difference:

For all have sinned, and come short of the glory of God; Being justified freely by his grace through the redemption that is in Christ Jesus: Whom God hath set forth to be a propitiation through faith in his blood, to declare his righteousness for the remission of sins that are past, through the forbearance of God; To declare, I say, at this time his righteousness: that he might be just, and the justifier of him which believeth in Jesus.

Romans 3:22-26

But God commendeth his love toward us, in that, while we were yet sinners, Christ died for us.

Romans 5:8

Neither as being lords over God's heritage, but being examples to the flock.

1 Peter 5:3

I am Demonstration

As believers, the person that we are is the demonstration of the Holy Spirit in our lives. How much have we been changed by the Holy Spirit? How much have we been used by the Holy Spirit?

I am the demonstration of God's love. God created me out of love. Man is the out-picturing of God's idea of love.

I am the demonstration of God's love with each divine attribute I express.

———◦———

For I have given you an example, that ye should do as I have done to you.
John 13:15

And my speech and my preaching was not with enticing words of man's wisdom, but in demonstration of the Spirit and of power:

That your faith should not stand in the wisdom of men, but in the power of God.
1 Corinthians 2:4-5

For even hereunto were ye called: because Christ also suffered for us, leaving us an example, that ye should follow his steps:
1 Peter 2:21

I Demonstrate

Manifesting the truth of God in our lives is an unconscious act of living. When we live the truth of God, this is the manifestation of God in us. We have become the demonstration of that truth. This truth is in turn demonstrated to the consciousness of others.

Demonstrating is also in the teaching of God's precepts. Paul explained to the people of Thessalonica the crucifixion and resurrection of Jesus was the same Christ spoke of in the Scriptures. Jesus, being the ultimate demonstration of love to mankind, was still a demonstration that was not self-evident, but needed explanation.

We, as believers in Jesus Christ, must also be that demonstration of salvation in word and deed. I demonstrate the life of Christ.

———

And Paul, as his manner was, went in unto them, and three sabbath days reasoned with them out of the scriptures, Opening and alleging, that Christ must needs have suffered, and risen again from the dead; and that this Jesus, whom I preach unto you, is Christ.

Acts 17:2-3

But have renounced the hidden things of dishonesty, not walking in craftiness, nor handling the word of God deceitfully; but by manifestation of the truth commending ourselves to every man's conscience in the sight of God.

2 Corinthians 4:2

Let no man despise thy youth; but be thou an example of the believers, in word, in conversation, in charity, in spirit, in faith, in purity.

1 Timothy 4:12

God is Forgiveness

The forgiveness of sin is a vital part of the Christian faith. Left to our own devices and proclivity to sin, our lives accumulate baggage and weight that is counterproductive to our spiritual health. Preaching the forgiveness of sins through Christ is the message of the gospel. It is this act of forgiveness by our Lord that allows us to lay claim to justification. Justification of man denotes the completed work of Christ. Justification by Christ means a verdict has been rendered in favor of the accused. God's forgiveness through Christ has declared man "justified" or blameless. No further indictments or judgments can be made.

Forgiveness of sin by God, not only means freeing man from his due recompense, but even more than that; enables him to receive the grace of God. This is not a benefit with limits. Forgiveness facilitates the Grace of God, which is available to man without measure.

———————

To the Lord our God belong mercies and forgivenesses, though we have rebelled against him;
Daniel 9:9

But he, whom God raised again, saw no corruption. Be it known unto you therefore, men and brethren, that through this man is preached unto you the forgiveness of sins: And by him all that believe are justified from all things, from which ye could not be justified by the law of Moses.
Acts 13:37-39

In whom we have redemption through his blood, the forgiveness of sins, according to the riches of his grace;
Ephesians 1:7

In whom we have redemption through his blood, even the forgiveness of sins:
Colossians 1:14

I am Forgiven

Confession is an act of contrition that assures us that God is listening, God knows, and God is responding to our requests. The truth is, all sin is forgiven. When Jesus declared, "It is finished" all sin that man had committed prior to the crucifixion was forgiven. At this same time, Jesus forgave the sins of all future generations. Those living today have committed their sins in the future, from the perspective of the cross. The good news is: all sin is forgiven now and forever, today and tomorrow, irrespective of time.

———◆———

I acknowledge my sin unto thee, and mine iniquity have I not hid. I said, I will confess my transgressions unto the Lord; and thou forgavest the iniquity of my sin. Selah.
Psalm 32:5

Verily I say unto you, All sins shall be forgiven unto the sons of men, and blasphemies wherewith soever they shall blaspheme:
Mark 3:28

I am Forgiving

It behooves us to show in like manner the forgiveness we have received of God. Just as in the "Lord's Prayer" we are to forgive those who trespass against us. Any neglect to forgive is duly noted and charged to our account, so to speak. We can't ask in good conscious for God to forgive us when we are withholding from others. If you enjoy holding a grudge toward someone who has done you wrong, God may not be so quick to lend ear to your needs, knowing that you have not done right by your brother.

To be a Christian is to be Christ-like, and to be Christ-like is to be forgiving one to another.

So shall ye say unto Joseph, Forgive, I pray thee now, the trespass of thy brethren, and their sin; for they did unto thee evil: and now, we pray thee, forgive the trespass of the servants of the God of thy father. And Joseph wept when they spake unto him.

Genesis 50:17

For if ye forgive men their trespasses, your heavenly Father will also forgive you:

Matthew 6:14

Whose soever sins ye remit, they are remitted unto them; and whose soever sins ye retain, they are retained.

John 20:23

And be ye kind one to another, tenderhearted, forgiving one another, even as God for Christ's sake hath forgiven you.

Ephesians 4:32

Forbearing one another, and forgiving one another, if any man have a quarrel against any: even as Christ forgave you, so also do ye.

Colossians 3:13

God is Love

Our God is a God of love and peace. Of all the attributes and all the truths that can be applied to God, first and foremost is the quality of love. All that is, is capsulized in love. The emotion that motivates God is love. All power that God exercises is directed by love. No matter the myriad of things God can do, nothing exceeds His ability to love. Love is the essence of God.

How does love behave?

Love does not want something that belongs to others. It rejoices in the goodness others receive. Love does not seek praise. It's desire is to praise. Love is not full of pride/inflated ego. It recognizes that all gifts and abilities are from God. Love does not mistreat others or show bigotry. It extends every courtesy to everyone, without partiality. Love is not selfish. It gives its time and energy to others. Love does not react in violent ways. Love is calm and confident in the face of adversity. Love does not wish ill will toward others. It desires only Good for others (success and prosperity). Love does not revel in wrongdoing. It rejoices in blessing others.

Demonstrating love is paramount in all that we do. If you have trouble grasping what it means to love, read and reread 1 Corinthians 13.

Finally, brethren, farewell. Be perfect, be of good comfort, be of one mind, live in peace; and the God of love and peace shall be with you.

2 Corinthians 13:11

He that loveth not knoweth not God; for God is love.

1 John 4:8

I am Loved

Pure love is merciful. It does not require love in return. God's love for man is unconditional. God has never required man to prove himself or to do any thing to be deserving of His love. God, by His very nature loves. God cannot, not love.

I am loved because of who God is, not because of who I am.

I am the prime focus of God's love and attention.

⟶❖⟵

The Lord hath appeared of old unto me, saying, Yea, I have loved thee with an everlasting love: therefore with lovingkindness have I drawn thee.

Jeremiah 31:3

For God so loved the world, that he gave his only begotten Son, that whosoever believeth in him should not perish, but have everlasting life.

John 3:16

Greater love hath no man than this, that a man lay down his life for his friends.

John 15:13

But God, who is rich in mercy, for his great love wherewith he loved us,

Ephesians 2:4

We love him, because he first loved us.

1 John 4:19

I am Loving

We are compelled to love when we experience God's love.

Even when we do not feel love toward another God reminds us we need to show love to that person. In fact, we are commanded to love one another. In doing so we are fulfilling the law of God. In a manner of speaking, loving our neighbor is the highest expression of love, even greater (if it were possible) than keeping the whole of the Ten Commandments.

As the servants of God we should honor all men, love the brotherhood, and fear God.

———————

A new commandment I give unto you, That ye love one another; as I have loved you, that ye also love one another.

John 13:34

Owe no man any thing, but to love one another: for he that loveth another hath fulfilled the law.

Romans 13:8

Seeing ye have purified your souls in obeying the truth through the Spirit unto unfeigned love of the brethren, see that ye love one another with a pure heart fervently:

1Peter 1:22

For this is the love of God, that we keep his commandments: and his commandments are not grievous.

1 John 5:3

God is Mercy

God's Mercy is in withholding our just dues. God does not forsake us because of being unworthy. Neither does God destroy us in retribution for our transgressions. God's mercy is required by His love for man. God with impunity, staves immediate judgment at the time sin is committed.

No less than 41 times in the Old Testament, it is said of God, "His mercy endures forever."

———>●<———

(For the Lord thy God is a merciful God;) he will not forsake thee, neither destroy thee, nor forget the covenant of thy fathers which he sware unto them. Deuteronomy 4:31

For if ye turn again unto the Lord, your brethren and your children shall find compassion before them that lead them captive, so that they shall come again into this land: for the Lord your God is gracious and merciful, and will not turn away his face from you, if ye return unto him. 2 Chronicles 30:9

Gracious is the Lord, and righteous; yea, our God is merciful. Psalm 116:5

And rend your heart, and not your garments, and turn unto the Lord your God: for he is gracious and merciful, slow to anger, and of great kindness, and repenteth him of the evil. Joel 2:13

But God, who is rich in mercy, for his great love wherewith he loved us, Ephesians 2:4

Grace be with you, mercy, and peace, from God the Father, and from the Lord Jesus Christ, the Son of the Father, in truth and love. 2 John 1:3

I receive Mercy

Eight times the Psalmist appeals to the Lord "Be merciful to me." Psalm 26:11, 41:4, 41:10, 56:1, 57:1, 86:3, 119:58 and 119:132. This is an example prayer to God. This is man's plea for help that only God can answer. This is an example of how God's mercy works in the lives of men.

Those who are truly repentant seek God's mercy.

We must depend on God's mercy to stay focused on what is important and not give up hope.

———————————

Surely goodness and mercy shall follow me all the days of my life: and I will dwell in the house of the Lord for ever.

Psalm 23:6

And the publican, standing afar off, would not lift up so much as his eyes unto heaven, but smote upon his breast, saying, God be merciful to me a sinner.

Luke 18:13

Therefore seeing we have this ministry, as we have received mercy, we faint not;

2 Corinthians 4:1

I am Merciful

It is good that I show mercy to others. It is a requirement that I love mercy, and to offer it without any mental reservation or secret evasion of mind.

If you want to do right by others ensure that you show mercy. True justice employs both mercy and compassion.

After giving the account of the Samaritan who cared for a man who had been beaten and robbed, Jesus also gave the simple and direct admonition to "go and do likewise." This is an example of what is means to love your neighbor: showing mercy.

———⟫●⟪———

The merciful man doeth good to his own soul: but he that is cruel troubleth his own flesh.

Proverbs 11:17

He hath shewed thee, O man, what is good; and what doth the Lord require of thee, but to do justly, and to love mercy, and to walk humbly with thy God?

Micah 6:8

Thus speaketh the Lord of hosts, saying, Execute true judgment, and shew mercy and compassions every man to his brother:

Zachariah 7:9

And he said, He that shewed mercy on him. Then said Jesus unto him, Go, and do thou likewise.

Luke 10:37

God is Provision

Jehovah-jireh – Jehovah will provide.

God is my all-providing Source. Divine Mind is the all-providing activity of my supply.

There are no less than 5 verses in the Bible that speak of God's promise to "provide atonement." Deuteronomy 21:8, 32:43, 2 Chronicles 30:18, Psalm 65:3, 79:9.

———⟫●⟪———

And Abraham said, My son, God will provide himself a lamb for a burnt offering: so they went both of them together.
Genesis 22:8

And Abraham called the name of that place Jehovahjireh: as it is said to this day, In the mount of the Lord it shall be seen.
Genesis 22:14

And it came to pass, because the midwives feared God, that he made them houses.
Exodus 1:21

For the Lord hath chosen Zion; he hath desired it for his habitation. This is my rest for ever: here will I dwell; for I have desired it. I will abundantly bless her provision: I will satisfy her poor with bread.
Psalm 132:13-15

And it shall be to me a name of joy, a praise and an honour before all the nations of the earth, which shall hear all the good that I do unto them: and they shall fear and tremble for all the goodness and for all the prosperity that I procure unto it.
Jeremiah 33:9

I am Proviso
I am provided for

God uses the most unlikely means to provide for our basic needs. In the case of Elijah, God arranged for him to be fed bread and meat in the morning and evening, delivered to him by ravens.

Even a person who seemingly has little, God is able to use in a mighty way. God arranged for a widow who lived in Zarephath to provide Elijah with sustenance. The widow did not refuse to help but noted that her recourses alone seemed inadequate for the three. She prepared bread for the prophet Elijah first. After that, she made bread for herself and her son. "For thus says the Lord God of Israel: The bin of flour shall not be used up, nor shall the jar of oil run dry, until the day the Lord sends rain on the earth."
1 Kings 17:14

Arise, get thee to Zarephath, which belongeth to Zidon, and dwell there: behold, I have commanded a widow woman there to sustain thee. 1 Kings 17:9

The Lord is my shepherd; I shall not want. Psalm 23:1

The young lions do lack, and suffer hunger: but they that seek the Lord shall not want any good thing.
Psalm 34:10

Are not two sparrows sold for a farthing? and one of them shall not fall on the ground without your Father. But the very hairs of your head are all numbered. Fear ye not therefore, ye are of more value than many sparrows.
Matthew 10:29-31

Thinkest thou that I cannot now pray to my Father, and he shall presently give me more than twelve legions of angels?
Matthew 26:53

I am Provider

Providing for family is everyone's first responsibility. Even seeming acts of charity are wrong, if you have denied care for your family. "To do justice and judgment is more acceptable to the Lord than sacrifice." Proverbs 21:3

———➤●◄———

And Joseph nourished his father, and his brethren, and all his father's household, with bread, according to their families.
Genesis 47:12

Pass through the host, and command the people, saying, Prepare you victuals; for within three days ye shall pass over this Jordan, to go in to possess the land, which the Lord your God giveth you to possess it.
Joshua 1:11

And Solomon had twelve officers over all Israel, which provided victuals for the king and his household: each man his month in a year made provision.
1 Kings 4:7

And he dealt wisely, and dispersed of all his children throughout all the countries of Judah and Benjamin, unto every fenced city: and he gave them victual in abundance. And he desired many wives.
2 Chronicles 11:23

She riseth also while it is yet night, and giveth meat to her household, and a portion to her maidens.
Proverbs 31:15

But if any provide not for his own, and specially for those of his own house, he hath denied the faith, and is worse than an infidel.
1 Timothy 5:8

God is Sacrifice

God established the idea of sacrifice of self and sacrifice for sin.

Abraham assured his son Isaac, that God would provide the needed burnt offering (sacrifice). "And Abraham said, My son, God will provide himself a lamb for a burnt offering: so they went both of them together." Genesis 22:8

———————

The sacrifices of God are a broken spirit: a broken and a contrite heart, O God, thou wilt not despise.

Psalm 51:17

And walk in love, as Christ also hath loved us, and hath given himself for us an offering and a sacrifice to God for a sweetsmelling savour.

Ephesians 5:2

By him therefore let us offer the sacrifice of praise to God continually, that is, the fruit of our lips giving thanks to his name. But to do good and to communicate forget not: for with such sacrifices God is well pleased.

Hebrews 13:15-16

Ye also, as lively stones, are built up a spiritual house, an holy priesthood, to offer up spiritual sacrifices, acceptable to God by Jesus Christ.

1Peter 2:5

I am Sacrificial

Paul reminds us that for believers, Christ is the manifestation of the Passover. Christ is the realization of the metaphor of Gods covering for sin: the blood of the Passover Lamb. Man is the recipient of this covering. Man is the reason for Christ's sacrifice. When Jesus declared, "It is finished" He forever put to rest the need of sacrifice for sin.

———

Purge out therefore the old leaven, that ye may be a new lump, as ye are unleavened. For even Christ our passover is sacrificed for us:
1 Corinthians 5:7

And walk in love, as Christ also hath loved us, and hath given himself for us an offering and a sacrifice to God for a sweetsmelling savour.
Ephesians 5:2

But this man, after he had offered one sacrifice for sins for ever, sat down on the right hand of God;
Hebrews 10:12

I am Sacrificing

Man can no more sacrifice for himself than he can save himself. Any sacrifice is not for self, but for others.

Whatever time we devote to our faith is sacrificial to God.

Whatever time we devote to man is sacrificing our good to others. We have a finite amount of time on earth. The more time we spend for God and the good of others, the less selfish we will be. I am sacrificing my life for good.

I will offer to thee the sacrifice of thanksgiving, and will call upon the name of the Lord.

Psalm 116:17

Let my prayer be set forth before thee as incense; and the lifting up of my hands as the evening sacrifice.

Psalm 141:2

I beseech you therefore, brethren, by the mercies of God, that ye present your bodies a living sacrifice, holy, acceptable unto God, which is your reasonable service.

Romans 12:1

Ye also, as lively stones, are built up a spiritual house, an holy priesthood, to offer up spiritual sacrifices, acceptable to God by Jesus Christ.

1 Peter 2:5

CHAPTER 5

Contemplative Prayer

Putting Attributes to Action

Now that we have pondered many attributes of God and man, it is incumbent upon us to turn this knowledge into praxis. Learning and never implementing what you have learned is akin to insanity. One could possibly be better off never having learned at all as to know truth and neglect it. As James 4:17 teaches us "Therefore to him that knoweth to do good, and doeth it not, to him it is sin."

These attributes need to be recited daily and established as a matter of rote memory. This is the best way of internalizing who God is and who you are.

In his book on <u>Creative Meditation</u>, Carlton Whitehead teaches us to clarify our beliefs about the nature of God.

"Think about the reality that 'Mind is one,' 'God is one,' that there is only one creating Intelligence, until the light of this truth begins to shine in your consciousness, dissolving the darkness of duality. Even clearer becomes the realization of one source, one intelligence, one power, universally present here and now. Contemplate the nature of this Oneness existing as the all-pervading and ever-present qualities of Life, Love, Light, Power, Peace Beauty, and Joy. Let your awareness of these qualities come alive."

These are the some of the same qualities that have already been presented. Even so, the several more offered in previous chapters, is not to suggest you have been given an exhaustive list of God's attributes. There are more to be discovered.

In his book <u>Treatment, What it is and how to do it</u>, Raymond Charles Barker gives further insight in defining the Nature of God.

"Make statements about God. Declare what you believe God to be in your own terms. Write out a list of synonyms for God. Speak these definitions aloud and rapidly as often as you can. – By defining God and lengthening your list daily you are soon able to build a vocabulary to describe God, the Good, Omnipotent. Words are important. Get a flow and an ease in making audible statements of Truth."

The faith we exercise is based on our monotheistic belief in God. The Jewish faith is grounded in the Shema Yisrael "Hear, O Israel: the LORD our God, the LORD is one" as found in Deuteronomy 6:4.

In Mark 12:29-30 we find the New Testament teaching of the same commandment. "And Jesus answered him, The first of all the commandments is, Hear, O Israel; The Lord our God is one Lord: And thou shalt love the Lord thy God with all thy heart, and with all thy soul, and with all thy mind, and with all thy strength: this is the first commandment."

A lawyer of the Pharisees tested Jesus with "Master, which is the great commandment in the law? Jesus said unto him, Thou shalt love the Lord thy God with all thy heart, and with all thy soul, and with all thy mind. This is the first and great commandment. And the second is like unto it, Thou shalt love thy neighbour as thyself. Matthew 22:36-39

Even the Christian construct of the Trinity is reliant on the teaching of the Shema. "For there are three that bear record in heaven, the Father, the Word, and the Holy Ghost: and these three are one. And there are three that bear witness in earth, the Spirit, and the water, and the blood: and these three agree in one." 1 John 5:7-8

Our challenge then, is to know this One God for who He is and what He has purposed for us. Our plot in life is to know God and "the glory of His Majesty."

There is no need for waiting for a new dispensation. We needn't bother looking for a sign of the times. Jesus said "behold, now is the accepted time; behold, now is the day of salvation.)"

2 Corinthians 6:2b

There is no room for shame and embarrassment.

"Whosoever therefore shall be ashamed of me and of my words in this adulterous and sinful generation; of him also shall the Son of man be ashamed, when he cometh in the glory of his Father with the holy angels." Mark 8:38

"For whosoever shall be ashamed of me and of my words, of him shall the Son of man be ashamed, when he shall come in his own glory, and in his Father's, and of the holy angels." Luke 9:26

Are you living for today or for tomorrow?

What you do with this information depends on your understanding of life on earth with respect to that which is to come. Take care not to fall into the dispensational trap. Those who do, risk becoming apathetic concerning the here and now. They have their eyes on their reward in heaven, having prayed a prayer escaping the everlasting torments of hell. They are those biding their time until their last breath is taken and they are suddenly in the presence of the Lord. What about now? Is life as a Christian worth any effort above that of a non-believer?

The following tables contain the same attributes that were covered in chapters 2-4. The idea is to study these and commit as many to memory as possible. When you are working with the reflective and reciprocal lists, preface each attribute with "I am becoming" until you are confident in saying, "I am" before each attribute. This will allow you to start quickly without any hesitations. Once you have established these truths as part of your belief system, you will find that prayer becomes a joy, not a chore; and asking for any needs or desires to be acted upon are God's good pleasure to fulfill.

Symbiotic Attributes

GOD IS	I AM
Atonement	Atoneable
Begetter	Begotten
Covenant	Covenantal
Fulfillment	Fulfilled
Government	Governable
Guidance	Guided
Head of the church	Body of the church
Judge	Judged
Justifying	Justified
Liberty	Liberated
Maintainer	Maintainable
Ordainer	Ordained
Potter	Clay
Praised	Praising
Revelation	Revelational
Satisfaction	Satisfied
Thankfulness	Thanksgiving

Reflective Attributes

GOD IS	I AM
Abundance	Abundant
Almightiness	Mighty
Beauty	Beautiful
Christ	Christ-like
Commitment	Committed
Compassion	Compassionate
Completeness	Complete
Confidence	Confident
Delights in	Delight in
Discernment	Discerning
Empowerment	Empowered
Eternity	Eternal
Faithfulness	Faithful
Freedom	Free
Generosity	Generous
Giver	Giving
Glory	Glorified
Goodness	Good
Grace	Gracious
Health	Healthy
Holiness	Holy
Honor	Honorable
Hope	Hopeful
Joy	Joyful
Justice	Just
Kindness	Kind
Knowledge	Knowing
Life	Living
Light	Light

Mind	Mind
Order	Ordered
Peace	Peaceable
Perfection	Perfect
Pleasure	Pleasing
Plenty	Plentiful
Power	Powerful
Prosperity	Prosperous
Pureness	Pure
Rejoicer	Rejoiceful
Riches	Rich
Righteousness	Righteous
Spirit	Spirit
Strength	Strong
Substance	Substance
Truth	Truthful
Understanding	Understanding
Wealth	Wealthy
Wisdom	Wise
Witness	Witnessing
Wholeness	Whole

Reciprocal Attributes

God IS	I AM (receive)	I AM (give)
Blessing	Blessed	Bless
Comforter	Comforted	Comforting
Demonstrator	Demonstration	Demonstrating
Forgiveness	Forgiven	Forgiving
Love	Loved	Loving
Mercy	Mercy	Merciful
Provision	Proviso	Provider
Sacrifice	Sacrificial	Sacrificing

Misnomers And Misconceptions

It is important for us to be able to recognize and dispel false teachings. For instance, belief in prevention is a false hope. A frequently asked question after experiencing disaster is "Why didn't God prevent that?" This is to suggest that God is less than Himself lacking in power to intervene, or lacking the love to care for those who are affected. This is simply an excuse used by individuals to deny Gods place in their lives. "You did not do what I wanted so I'm not going to serve you." Do you see the pettiness in this response?

The truth of the matter is, God is <u>not</u> in the <u>prevention</u> business. The word prevention is only used in the Bible 7 times. And none of those times is it used as an attribute ascribed to God. God as a stopgap is the fantasy of mankind. God <u>is</u> in the <u>protection</u> business. He does not prevent the storm from occurring; He protects us in the storm. Jesus did not prevent the ensuing storm from coming. He demonstrated God's protection in the storm. God is our protector. Man is the protected.

Wouldn't it be ludicrous for someone to claim their joy was in knowing that God prevented an airplane from crashing into their house, a tornado hitting their house, or fire burning it to the ground every day? How would anyone know these were even possibilities for the day? If this were the case, we could occupy our time constructing long lists of bad things God prevented. The whole problem with prevention is you can't know for sure what could have happened but didn't.

This is to illustrate the importance of, in practicing your faith, to speak only affirmations that are true. Take care not to succumb to cliché or common false beliefs simply because they sound religious. Speaking of Jews of Berea, Paul reported "These were more noble than those in Thessalonica, in that they received the word with all readiness of mind, and searched the scriptures daily, whether those things were so." (Acts 17:11) We should do likewise.

The affirmations provided in this writing have been carefully researched, and reflect the truth of God and the truth of man according to the scriptures. It is important that we apply these and others to be discovered, to conscious thought. To neglect the attributes of God and man is akin to denying them. Jesus said in

Matthew 10:33 "But whosoever shall deny me before men, him will I also deny before my Father which is in heaven."

Practice what you have learned

The difference between someone who is newly accomplished and one who is considered to be a scholar is this: the accomplished works until he gets it right, the scholar continues to work until he can't get it wrong. It is the same in our walk with God. Don't just practice your faith until you do a good thing, and stop. Practice to the point that you never have to stop and ask yourself "Am I doing the right thing?" You don't need to spend hours evaluating and pondering. You don't need to take it to committee or even ask a friend. Practicing your faith is an extension of who you are. You, being one with God, know what is truth. You intrinsically know what is good. It was John Wesley who admonished his followers to "do all the good you can." I would to God that more men and women would take this sentiment to heart. Our heavenly task is to be immersed in the love of God: continually studying the love of God and learning how to demonstrate the love of God.

CHAPTER 6
Bringing Reality to Mind

The image of God / The Likeness of men, was borne out of the heartfelt concern for the state of affairs of this world we live in. With wars, rumors of war and conflicts in every corner of the globe, one can only wonder; is this really the way things should be? What can be done to restore order, bring peace and instill a sense of respect for all human life in this world?

A balanced belief system

It was John Wesley who gave us the construct of the quadrilateral. He determined that faith formation is influenced by four key sources: the Bible, reason, tradition and experience.

The Bible matters

The Bible is its own best proof of Divine authority. The claims within its pages are second to none.

"All scripture is given by inspiration of God, and is profitable for doctrine, for reproof, for correction, for instruction in righteousness: That the man of God may be perfect, thoroughly furnished unto all good works." 2 Timothy 3:16-17

"So shall my word be that goeth forth out of my mouth: it shall not return unto me void, but it shall accomplish that which I please, and it shall prosper in the thing whereto I sent it." Isaiah 55:11

"For the word of God is quick, and powerful, and sharper than any twoedged sword, piercing even to the dividing asunder of soul and spirit, and of the joints and marrow, and is a discerner of the thoughts and intents of the heart." Hebrews 4:12

"For precept must be upon precept, precept upon precept; line upon line, line upon line; here a little, and there a little:" Isaiah 28:10

"Thy word have I hid in mine heart, that I might not sin against thee." Psalm 119:11

"and there is no God else beside me; a just God and a Saviour; there is none beside me." Isaiah 45:21b

"Search the scriptures; for in them ye think ye have eternal life: and they are they which testify of me." John 5:39

"Jesus saith unto him, I am the way, the truth, and the life: no man cometh unto the Father, but by me." John 14:6

The understanding of scripture is influenced by whether an individual is predisposed toward a literal, metaphorical or metaphysical form of interpretation.

Reason matters

Your philosophy of life is shaped by reason. God has given man an analytical mind, which has served man well through the ages. Reason has spawned various philosophical schools of thought: the Empiricism of Bacon and Hume; the Existentialism of Kierkegaard; the Idealism of Dante; the Naturalism of Voltaire; the Nominalism of Occam; the Objectivism of Rand; the Perspectivism of Nietzsche; the Pragmatism of Dewey; the Rationalism of Hobbes, Locke and Spinoza, the Realism of Plato; the Scholasticism of Aristotle; the Subjective Idealism of Berkeley; the Transcendental Idealism of Kant; and the Transcendentalism of Emerson.

Your acquisition of knowledge is contingent on reason. Reason enables our use of the scientific method, which tests and proves the truth of nature and its laws.

It is with deductive reasoning that we can arrive at an answer through the narrowing down of probabilities (the process of elimination).

Reason gives us the principle of transitive properties, which we use in solving math problems. This same principle can be applied in discovering Bible truths.

Reason provides us with the rules of argumentation that present matters as a major premise, minor premise and conclusion; known as syllogism.

A-priori reasoning is relating knowledge that proceeds from theoretical deduction rather than from observation or experience.

The study of Hermeneutics generally relies on the inductive method of reasoning.

Each use of reason can be applied to Bible study; which correlates like terms, illustrates relational connections between Old and New Testament scriptures, and provides a framework for our belief system. Reason, illuminates what we have seen before and brings new truth to our minds.

Faith tradition matters

Whether it be the teachings of the, Judaism, the early Christian Church, Gnosticism, Roman Catholicism, Eastern Orthodoxy, the Protestant Reformation, Evangelicalism, Modernism, New Thought, Fundamentalism, Pentecostalism, Neo-Orthodoxy, or Progressivism: faith traditions matter. Faith traditions influence the way we think and respond to God in our world. Traditions solidify what we believe and demonstrate why these beliefs are valid. Beliefs that are the most valued are the traditions passed from generation to generation. While some faith traditions have remained intact, as others have faded, it is likely that new expressions of faith and worship will emerge.

Life experience matters

Our day-to-day experiences are the measure against all that we have learned. Our experiences either confirm or deny preconceptions. Experience that agrees with our knowledge validates it as truth. Experience that disagrees with our concept of reality causes conflict. This conflict can be resolved through examining the source of our belief. Either the source is in error or our understanding of it is in error. In this state, truth cannot exist. It is our task to exercise discernment, and to prove what is true.

Realizing life more abundantly
Putting things into perspective

Belief in Intelligent design matters

If people understood who they really were, a child of God, their behavior would be entirely different than what we see today. A person who has confidence in who they are (God's unique and special creation) behaves in a manner that is respectful toward his fellow man. Knowing that I am created in the image of God gives me a perspective on life that directs my attention to God and demands the proper treatment of others. No one can honestly say they love God and at the same time foster ill will toward his neighbor. Good and evil cannot abide in man at the same time.

Belief in one God matters

Too many are spending the precious time God has given to them to combat one another. Too many are seeking ways to knock someone else down in order to get a step ahead. Nations war against nations that a select few might "win" against others. This cannot be the way God intended man to live. These are merely indicators that man is in desperate need of divine intervention.

Knowing who God is matters

Identifying the attributes of God and meditating on them draws us closer to our creator. In doing so, we gain a healthy understanding of who God is and what our relationship with Him should be. When we learn who we are, we also gain a greater sense of life purpose. It is all a matter of internalizing what it means to be created in the image of God. As such, man will never know who he is until he first understands who God is. And it is only through the faith of Christ, that we may know God. Jesus said of himself that men should "learn of me."

Knowing who I am matters

When I know who I am in Christ, there is no time for backbiting, arguing and conflict. Having the mind of Christ is in internalizing His attributes. God mirrored many of His attributes in the creation of man. We need to discover what they are and exercise them.

My Life matters

Because of Jesus, we are reconciled to God, now and forever. The highest praise we can offer God is living a life that is a reflection of Christ. It is incumbent in this world that people know themselves to be "created in the image of God" and conduct themselves accordingly.

ABOUT THE AUTHOR

Through the past 35 years, Mr. McClerren has worked with AWANA clubs, conducted children's Sunday school classes, and taught adult Bible studies. He is Senior Pastor at Chicago Lawn United Methodist Church.

Mr. McClerren's undergraduate studies are in Education, his graduate studies in Theology, and postgraduate work in Religious Studies. He is a committed lifelong learner: a 21st century Renaissance man. Among his accomplishments are those of private pilot, missile technician and certified teacher.

Mr. McClerren has taught for San Diego City College, ITT Technical Institute and the University of Oklahoma. He served as education advisor for the Navy College Program, providing academic counseling for military personnel. He is also the Illinois State Representative for the Wolcott Foundation: an organization that awards fellowships for master's degree studies at George Washington University.

Mr. McClerren is an accomplished vocal musician. He has served as singing judge for the Barbershop Harmony Society. He has performed with choruses competing on the international stage; medaling twice. Mr. McClerren was tenor in "Take Note" quartet, while winning the Illinois District Senor Quartet Championship three consecutive years. He is also the tenor on the Christmas Grace recording by "A-Men" gospel quartet.

Mr. McClerren is married; and lives with his wife and daughter in Lake County Illinois.

Printed in the United States
By Bookmasters